The Many Veils of the Moon

A Grimoire of Lunar Magic for the Green Witch

The Many Veils of the Moon

A Grimoire of Lunar Magic for the Green Witch

Mitchell King

London, UK
Washington, DC, USA

First published by Moon Books, 2026
Moon Books is an imprint of Collective Ink Ltd.,
Unit 11, Shepperton House, 89 Shepperton Road, London, N1 3DF
office@collectiveinkbooks.com
www.collectiveinkbooks.com
www.moon-books.net

For distributor details and how to order please visit the 'Ordering' section on our website.

Text copyright: Mitchell King 2024

ISBN: 978 1 80341 994 7
978 1 78904 929 9 (ebook)
Library of Congress Control Number: 2024950120

All rights reserved. Except for brief quotations in critical articles or reviews, no part of this book may be reproduced in any manner without prior written permission from the publishers.

The rights of Mitchell King as author have been asserted in accordance with the Copyright, Designs and Patents Act 1988.

A CIP catalogue record for this book is available from the British Library.

Design: Lapiz Digital Services
Illustrated by Kay Savage

UK: Printed and bound by CPI Group (UK) Ltd, Croydon, CR0 4YY
US: Printed and bound by Thomson-Shore, 7300 West Joy Road, Dexter, MI 48130

We operate a distinctive and ethical publishing philosophy in all areas of our business, from our global network of authors to production and worldwide distribution.

Contents

Also by Mitchell King

The Mostly True Memoirs of a Witch
(9781950380930)

This grimoire is lovingly dedicated to my mother, Deborah Leigh Vealey-King, whose passionate character and profound love first opened my eyes to the magic in the world around me. She showed me the power in the moon's cycles, the enchantment in the natural world, and the strength that can be found even in the midst of life's greatest challenges. Even through her battle with cancer, she remained a beacon of light, guiding me with her love and magic.

One of my earliest "Books of Magic" was her worn, dog-eared copy of Love Signs by Linda Goodman. I thought astrology held all the answers for a while and that those pages contained the most powerful magic. Looking back, it was one of the first tools that sparked my journey into witchcraft. My mother passed down bits of charms and lore, little fragments of wisdom woven from her heritage and spirit. Those pieces of magic became a foundation for me, the roots of a road I try to walk with the same honesty and love as she did before me.

This book is also for my grandmother, Vivien Violet Gulick, who passed away when my mother was only fifteen. Though I never knew her, I have felt her presence in the stories my mother shared and in the magic that she left behind. Through them, I gathered the strands of magic they carried, weaving them into my practice.

So, to the Moon and all mothers, to the cunning and the kind, this grimoire is dedicated. It is a tribute to the legacy of love, wisdom, and magic passed down from generation to generation.

And, of course, to my beloved husband, Michael, my true-pointing star.

May all our roads lead us back to each other.

May their spirits walk with me as I continue this path,
Guiding my hands as I weave the magic they gave me.

The Many Veils of the Moon

A Grimoire of Lunar Magic for the Green Witch

A Collection of Nature-Aligned Spells, Potions, and Rituals for Health, Wellness, and Protection

This Grimoire serves as a guide for the Green Witch, who feels called to work with the light and shadow of the Moon. One who seeks to work in harmony with nature, drawing upon its innate power for healing, protection, beauty, and strength. The spells, potions, and rituals here honor the wild, ethically gathering materials and ensuring that our magic aligns with the rhythms of the earth.

Glossary of Terms

As you walk the Green Path and dive into the magic of the Twin Moons, it's helpful to have a guide to the unique terms and concepts that shape this magical system. These definitions will help you navigate the spells and philosophy embedded within this grimoire.

Twin Moons, or The Lattice of The Twin Moons

The Twin Moons, or The Lattice of The Twin Moons, are the two key phases of the moon – the Full Moon and the Dark Moon – that represent the balance between light and shadow in Green Witchcraft. These moons work together in harmony, symbolizing duality:

- The Full Moon represents light, radiance, manifestation, protection, and visibility. It is when magic for growth, illumination, and outward action is most powerful.
- The Dark Moon represents concealment, introspection, protection through shadow, and banishing. It is the time for withdrawing, working in secrecy, and performing magic for endings and dissolution. (The Dark Moon is often called the "New Moon" in almanacs, calendars, and non-witchcraft literature.)

Together, the Twin Moons form the backbone of many spells and rituals, offering a balanced approach to magic that draws upon both the seen and unseen forces of nature.

Malefica

Malefica refers to harmful or negative magic, curses, ill intentions, or malevolent spiritual forces. It is magic that seeks to cause harm or disruption, often created with destructive intent. In Green Witchcraft, Malefica is acknowledged as a force that exists in the world, and certain spells (such as banishments or curses) may be necessary to deal with it. However, Green Witches typically use their magic defensively, preferring to reflect or dissolve Malefica, rather than seeking opportunities to harm others.

The Green Path

The Green Path is the spiritual and magical journey followed by the Green Witch. It is a path deeply connected to nature, the cycles of the moon, the seasons, and the earth itself. Witches walking the Green Path work in harmony with the forces of nature, seeking balance, healing, and protection. This path often involves foraging, herbal magic, plant-tending, and working with the elements of earth, water, air, and fire.

The Green Path is not a path of conquest or control, but one of nurturing, understanding, and living in alignment with natural cycles. It includes a deep respect for the wild, the unseen, and the powers that exist in the world.

Green Witch

A Green Witch is a practitioner of magic whose craft is rooted in nature and the earth. Green Witches are caretakers of the natural world, often working with plants, herbs, stones, and the cycles of the moon to craft spells and rituals. Their magic is tied to the seasons, the elements, and the rhythms of the earth. They honor the land, the wild creatures, and the spirits that dwell in nature, often acting as guardians or stewards of the places they inhabit.

Unlike some other forms of witchcraft, the Green Witch focuses more on harmony with nature and subtle magic that aligns with the earth's natural energy, rather than grand or elaborate rituals. Their power comes from their connection to the natural world and their ability to work with the resources the earth provides.

Athame

The Athame is a ceremonial dagger used in many magical practices, including Green Witchcraft. While the Athame is never used to cut physical objects, it is a powerful tool for directing energy, casting circles, and cutting energetic ties. In the Twin Moons system, the Athame is often used in the Dark Moon rites to sever harmful connections, break curses, or dissolve Malefica. It is a symbol of both power and protection, a tool that sharpens the witch's will and intent.

The Witch's Broom

The Witch's Broom (or besom) is a sacred tool used for cleansing and purifying spaces, sweeping away negative energy, and creating protective boundaries. In Green Witchcraft, the broom is a practical and symbolic tool. It is often used to sweep the area before rituals, clearing it of stagnant or harmful energy. The Witch's Broom can also be used during rituals of banishment, such as in the Rite of the Hollow Moon, to sweep away Malefica and harmful influences.

Full Moon Water & New Moon Water

Full Moon Water and Dark Moon Water are integral components of many spells in Green Witchcraft. These waters are charged with the energy of their respective lunar phases and used to anoint, cleanse, or empower tools, charms, or the witch themselves.

- Full Moon Water: Collected under the light of the Full Moon, this water carries the energy of manifestation, protection, growth, and illumination. It is often used to bless or anoint objects meant to be seen, empowered, or strengthened.
- Dark Moon Water: Collected under the Dark Moon, this water is imbued with the power of concealment, protection, and introspection. It is used to anoint charms or tools for secrecy, protection, or banishing spells.

The Structure of Spellcasting

In Green Witchcraft, the structure of a spell is just as important as the intent behind it. Spells require a reliable form that guides the witch through each phase of magical work - this form allows the energy to flow smoothly and ensures that the spell is cast with purpose and clarity. In this book, each spell follows a familiar pattern designed to help both the seasoned practitioner and the initiate navigate the rituals with confidence and incorporate them into their craft.

This framework is divided into three main stages: Casting the Circle, Invoking the Spell, and Sealing the Spell. Each step carries its own significance, rooted in the balance of nature and the Twin Moons – providing protection, focusing intention, and releasing magic into the world.

1. Casting the Circle: Preparing Sacred Space

Before any magic can be worked, the space must be prepared and protected. This step involves Casting the Circle, which creates a boundary between the witch and the outside world, ensuring that no harmful energies can interfere with the ritual. It is a moment to center the mind, ground the energy, and ensure that the area is cleansed and free of distractions.

Tools for Casting the Circle:

- The Witch's Broom (used to sweep away negative or stagnant energy, clearing the space for ritual).
- Full Moon Water (to purify and bless the area).
- Salt or Herbs (for further protection and grounding).

This step is about more than just physical preparation - it is a symbolic act of setting your intention and focus. The circle represents the wholeness of nature and the balance you aim to create during the spell. As you sweep or sprinkle water, you are clearing the way for magic to flow.

2. Invoking the Spell: Calling the Energy

Once the circle is cast, the Invoking stage begins. This is where the magic truly happens. The witch calls upon the energies of the Twin Moons, the elements, or other forces depending on the nature of the spell. Here, the intent is stated clearly, and the focus is on directing the energy toward the desired outcome.

During this stage, the witch might use incantations or chants, symbolic actions, and magical tools to draw in the power needed for the spell.

Tools for Invoking the Spell:

- The Athame (for directing energy and cutting ties).
- Water or Fire (depending on whether the spell requires cleansing, protection, or transformation).
- Moon-charged objects (such as Full Moon Water, New Moon Water, or a reflective mirror).

This phase is the heart of the spell, where the witch's will meets the energy of nature. It's a time for visualization, calling forth the powers of the moon, and feeling the connection between yourself and the forces you are invoking. The energy is raised and focused toward your intention.

3. Sealing the Spell: Locking the Magic in Place

The final stage is Sealing the Spell. After the energy has been raised and the intent set, it is crucial to ground that energy and close the ritual. This ensures that the spell's magic is released into the world or locked in place, depending on its purpose, without leaving residual energy behind. Sealing also protects you from any lingering forces or unintended effects.

Tools for Sealing the Spell:

- Salt or earth (to ground and purify the remaining energy).
- Extinguishing candles (to release the energy safely).
- The Witch's Broom (to sweep the circle closed and ensure protection after the spell).

By sealing the spell, the witch completes the cycle of magic – what was called forth has been put into motion, and what was needed is now at rest. This final step ensures that the energy is properly grounded and that the spell is released to work in its own time.

Understanding the Flow of Magic

This three-step process is designed to help witches, whether new or experienced, maintain focus and flow throughout spell work. Each part of the ritual has a distinct purpose:

- Casting the Circle ensures protection and focus.
- Invoking the Spell is the act of raising and directing magical energy.
- Sealing the Spell grounds and protects, ensuring the energy is properly released.

This structure mirrors the natural balance that Green Witches strive for, aligning with the cycles of the Twin Moons and the energies of the Earth. By following this format, you work in harmony with the rhythms of nature, creating spells that are both powerful and safe.

A Ritual Framework for the Green Witch

Whether you are performing a protective charm, a glamour, or a curse, the structure of Casting, Invoking, and Sealing forms the backbone of every spell in the Green Witch's Grimoire. It ensures that you, as a witch, are in control of the energy you raise, and that your spells are carefully focused and grounded.

As you walk the Green Path, let this structure guide your magic, allowing you to work with the cycles of the Earth and the Twin Moons to create powerful, effective, and balanced spells.

The Cauldron of the Twin Moons

Creating Moon Water and Empowering Charms

The cauldron, a symbol of transformation, rebirth, and magical brewing, is a powerful vessel in your ritual work. In this spell, the cauldron is used to create both Full Moon and Dark Moon Water, drawing upon the balance of light and shadow, and as a resting place for charms and magical tools to secure the fulfillment of your spells.

You Will Need:

- A cauldron (or a large bowl if you do not have a cauldron)
- Spring water or natural, purified water
- A white candle for the Full Moon
- A black candle for the New Moon
- A piece of silver jewelry or a charm representing your intention
- Herbs for charging the water (optional, corresponding to your intention)

    - Rosemary for protection
    - Lavender for peace
    - Basil for abundance

Part 1: Creating Full Moon Water

The Full Moon Water harnesses the illuminating power of the Full Moon to charge the water with energy for clarity, purification, and manifestation.

1. Prepare the Cauldron: On the night of the Full Moon, place the cauldron outdoors or near a window where

the moonlight can touch it. Fill the cauldron with spring water, enough to submerge small charms or magical tools.

2. Light the White Candle: Light a white candle beside the cauldron, symbolizing the light and power of the Full Moon. As you light the candle, say:

   "By light of moon, both full and bright,
   I call your power, this sacred night.
   By water clear and flame's pure sight,
   Bless this vessel, with your might."

3. Empower the Water: Hold your hands over the cauldron and visualize the moon's light filling the water, charging it with purity and strength. You may add herbs to the water, depending on your intention (such as rosemary for protection or basil for abundance). As you focus your energy, chant:

   "By silver light and water clear,
   The moon's bright power, I draw near.
   By flame and star, by night and sea,
   This water's blessed, so mote it be."

4. Place a Charm Inside the Cauldron: Once the water is charged, place a piece of silver jewelry or a charm in the cauldron, allowing it to rest in the Full Moon Water overnight. This secures the charm with the energy of the moon, empowering it for future spell work.

Part 2: Creating Dark Moon Water

Dark Moon Water is created under the dark sky of the Dark Moon and carries the energy of renewal, concealment, and shadow work. It is particularly useful for spells of protection, banishment, or when working with hidden forces.

1. Prepare the Cauldron: On the night of the Dark Moon, fill the cauldron with spring water once again, placing it in a quiet, dark space where you can focus without interruption.
2. Light the Black Candle: Light a black candle beside the cauldron to represent the dark power of the Dark Moon, focusing on its energy for transformation, protection, and shadow work. Say:

   "By moon unseen and sky so deep,
   I call your power, while shadows creep.
   By water's flow and flame's dark sight,
   Bless this vessel, by shadow's might."

3. Empower the Water: As you did with the Full Moon Water, hold your hands over the cauldron and visualize the dark, still energy of the Dark Moon filling the water. Imagine it carrying the power of concealment and protection. As you focus, chant:

   "By moon of dark and water's flow,
   The power of shadows, I now know.
   By flame and night, by hidden sea,
   This water's blessed, so mote it be."

4. Place a Charm Inside the Cauldron: Just as with the Full Moon Water, place a charm or magical item inside the cauldron to infuse it with the Dark Moon's energy. Let it rest in the water overnight to absorb the protective and transformative powers of the Dark Moon.

Part 3: Empowering Charms in the Cauldron

The cauldron can be used as a resting place for charms, poppets, or herb bundles, allowing them to draw on the energy of either the Full Moon or the Dark Moon. This practice ensures that the spell's fulmination is sealed and secure.

1. Rest Charms in the Cauldron: After creating Full Moon Water or Dark Moon Water, allow your charms, poppets, or herb bundles to rest within the cauldron overnight, absorbing the lunar energy. The water acts as a magical conductor, empowering the objects for future use.
2. Recite the Final Incantation: Once the items have been placed in the cauldron, recite the following incantation to seal the magic:

   "In moon's deep light or shadow's grace,
   This charm is sealed in sacred space.
   By cauldron's edge, by water's power,
   The spell is set, it finds its hour."

Working with the Cauldron

The cauldron is a powerful tool for magical transformation and enchantment. By creating both Full Moon Water and Dark Moon Water in the cauldron, you tap into the balance of light and dark, ensuring your spells are charged with the right energy. Additionally, placing charms within the cauldron allows them to rest in sacred water, becoming potent vessels for magical work. Whether you seek clarity and illumination through the Full Moon or protection and concealment through the Dark Moon, the cauldron acts as the heart of your magical practice.

Rite of the Green Path

An Initiation

This self-initiation ritual is a sacred step, marking the beginning of the witch's journey down the Green Path – the hidden road that connects the witch with the forces of nature, the cycles of the moon, and the deep mysteries of the earth. It is a powerful rite that requires no tools beyond the witch, the Full Moon, the Dark Moon, and a secluded space where the veil between self and the natural world becomes thin.

The ritual is divided into two parts: the first under the Full Moon, when the witch is anointed with the light and energy of protection and openness to the natural world, and the second under the Dark Moon, when the witch is anointed with the power of concealment, silence, and the unseen mysteries. Together, these twin energies will seal the witch's initiation into Green Witchcraft, aligning them with both radiant and shadowed forces.

Part 1: The Full Moon Anointing – The Lighted Path

The Full Moon marks the beginning of your journey, illuminating the first steps onto the Green Path. Under the moon's radiant light, you will be anointed and blessed with protection and guidance as you step into the magic of the natural world.

You Will Need:

- A bowl of spring water (blessed under the Full Moon)
- A secluded outdoor space where you can see the moon or feel its presence

Instructions:

1. Find a Secluded Space Under the Full Moon: On the night of the Full Moon, find a quiet, secluded space where the moon's light can reach you, either directly or through its energy. Stand in silence for a moment, feeling the connection between yourself and the earth beneath your feet.
2. Prepare for the Anointing: Hold the bowl of spring water in both hands, lifting it gently toward the moon as if offering it to the sky. Let the moon's energy bless the water, imbuing it with protection, light, and the power to reveal the hidden road ahead of you.
3. The Anointing: Dip your fingers into the blessed water, and gently anoint your forehead, chest, and hands with the water, saying:

"By moon's bright light, I bless this night,
I walk the path of nature's sight.
By leaf, by root, by star, by stone,
The hidden road shall be my own."

4. As you speak, feel the moonlight surrounding you, forming a protective barrier that will guide you on your path and connect you to the forces of the wild.
5. Invocation of the Full Moon: Stand tall under the moon's gaze, open your arms to the sky, and feel the thrill of beginning this journey. Call out to the Full Moon, inviting its protection and guidance:

"By moon so full, by night so clear,
I call the wild, I cast off fear.
By herb, by tree, by water's flow,
Upon this path, I seek to grow."

Let the words vibrate through you, feeling the resonance of your voice and the energy of the moon working in harmony. In this moment, you are bound to the moon, open to its radiant guidance.

1. Close the First Half of the Rite: Close your eyes and take a deep breath, feeling the moon's protection settle around you. Whisper a final blessing to yourself:

   "The light shall guide, the wild shall show,
   Upon the Green Path, I shall go."

Part 2: The Dark Moon Anointing – The Hidden Path

The Dark Moon marks the second phase of your initiation, sealing you with the power of the hidden road – the road of silence, shadow, and unseen magic. As the moon withdraws into darkness, you shall be hidden, protected from Malefica, and shielded from harm.

You Will Need:

- A bowl of spring water (blessed under the New Moon)
- The same secluded outdoor space used during the Full Moon ritual

Instructions:

1. Find a Secluded Space Under the Dark Moon: On the night of the Dark Moon, return to the same space where you performed the Full Moon anointing. Stand in silence, feeling the presence of the dark sky above and the earth beneath your feet. Though the moon is hidden, its energy is still present – quiet and protective.

2. Prepare for the Anointing: Hold the bowl of Dark Moon water in your hands, lifting it to the sky. Though the moon is unseen, feel its dark power flow into the water, filling it with the energy of concealment, protection, and the deep mysteries of the earth.
3. The Anointing: Dip your fingers into the water and anoint yourself again – this time, focusing on your forehead, throat, and feet, the pathways of thought, voice, and movement. As you do, say:

   "By moon's dark veil, by shadow's grace,
   I walk unseen, I leave no trace.
   By root, by stone, by earth below,
   The hidden road I now shall know."

As you speak, feel the power of the Dark Moon enfolding you, concealing you from harm and guarding you as you step further into the Green Path.

1. Invocation of the Dark Moon: Stand still in the darkness, arms at your sides, allowing the quiet of the night to settle around you. Whisper to the Dark Moon:

   "By shadow's veil, by night so still,
   I call the dark to shield my will.
   By tree, by wind, by water's night,
   Upon this path, I hide from sight."

Feel the words resonate through the darkness, as if the unseen forces of the night are acknowledging your presence. In this moment, you are shielded and unseen, walking the hidden road beneath the stars.

1. Close the Rite of the Twin Moons: Close your eyes and breathe deeply, allowing the dark energy of the Dark Moon to merge with the protective light of the Full Moon, forming a complete circle of power around you. Whisper a final blessing:

   "The light shall guard, the dark shall hide,
   Upon this path, I walk with pride."

Let the energy of the rite settle around you, sealing your initiation. You are now walking the Green Path, aligned with the forces of nature and the cycles of the moon.

Through this Self-Initiation and Anointing, you are bound to the moon's radiant and shadowed aspects, walking the Green Path with protection and insight. The twin blessings of the Full and Dark Moon guard and guide you as you begin your journey, balancing light and darkness in harmony with the natural world. From this point forward, you are a Green Witch, walking the hidden road of nature's magic.

The Twin Moons: The Balance of Radiance and Shadow

In Green Witchcraft, the cycles of the moon govern much of our magic, guiding us with their natural rhythms of growth, decline, and renewal. But it is the harmonious relationship between the Full Moon and the Dark Moon – the Twin Moons – that holds profound significance. These two phases, though opposites in light and energy, work together to create the balance essential to the Green Path, as outlined in this work. One cannot exist without the other; they are two faces of the same, and through them, the witch finds both protection and concealment, visibility and invisibility, and light and shadow, both without and within.

The Twin Moons offer a duality that governs the natural world: the radiance of the Full Moon, which empowers us with illumination, growth, and protection, and the concealment of the Dark Moon, which grants us invisibility, secrecy, and the quiet power of the unseen. These two energies – one of openness, the other of enshadowed mystery – shape the witch's magic and practice, providing tools for navigating both the known and the unknown.

The Full Moon: The Lighted Path

The Full Moon, radiant and powerful, governs the side of the Green Path that is illuminated, where everything is seen and understood. It is a time of growth, clarity, and manifestation, when the witch is most visible to the world and nature's energies are at their peak. Under the Full Moon, spells for protection, abundance, love, and healing are most effective, drawing on the moon's light to amplify the witch's intentions.

The Full Moon calls the witch to be open, to gather energy from the natural world, and to channel it outward. It is a time to call forth the wild forces of nature, to be in harmony with the cycles of growth and fertility. In this phase, the witch walks the Lighted Path, where they are guided by the moon's radiant light and protected by its brilliance.

Correspondences of the Full Moon:

- Element: Water, reflecting and flowing
- Energy: Manifestation, illumination, growth, protection
- Magical Focus: Spells for abundance, healing, love, and clarity
- Rituals: Charging tools, divination, personal empowerment
- Herbs: Rosemary, lavender, basil
- Crystals: Clear quartz, moonstone, selenite

The Full Moon, in its fullness, allows us to shine our light, to show the world who we are, and to gather the energies of the earth to fortify ourselves and our magic. But with this visibility comes vulnerability, and so the Twin Moons remind us that balance must be kept – light must give way to shadow.

The Dark Moon: The Hidden Path

The Dark Moon, dark and mysterious, is the moon of concealment and protection. It governs the side of the Green Path that is hidden, where the witch moves unseen, shielded by the absence of light. It is a time of introspection, secrecy, and renewal, when spells for banishing, protection, and inner work are most potent. Under the Dark Moon, the witch withdraws from the visible world, drawing strength from the shadows and preparing for the cycle of renewal.

The Dark Moon calls the witch to turn inward, to seek the quiet power of the unseen and to work in harmony with the forces of the earth that move in silence. It is a time to shield oneself, to conceal magic and intentions from prying eyes, and to let the hidden road unfold beneath your feet. In this phase, the witch walks the Hidden Path, guarded by the dark veil of the moon and protected by the forces of shadow.

Correspondences of the Dark Moon:

- Element: Earth, grounding and concealment
- Energy: Protection, renewal, invisibility, banishing
- Magical Focus: Spells for protection, banishing, shadow work, and rest
- Rituals: Cleansing, meditation, breaking bad habits, divination
- Herbs: Sage, mugwort, yarrow
- Crystals: Obsidian, black tourmaline, onyx

The Dark Moon's power lies in its silence, its ability to shield and protect, allowing the witch to move unseen, unnoticed by those who may seek to cause harm. The Hidden Path is one of quiet strength, offering the witch the opportunity to withdraw and regain power from the shadows.

The Balance of the Twin Moon

Together, the Twin Moons represent the harmony of opposites: the visible and the invisible, the light and the shadow, the seen and the unseen. To walk the Green Path is to recognize and embrace the balance between these two forces, understanding that neither can exist without the other. Magic is most powerful when the witch knows when to step into the light and when to retreat into shadow.

The Full Moon calls for outward action, for gathering strength and manifesting intentions, while the Dark Moon calls for inward reflection, for protection and quiet regeneration. As the moon cycles through these phases, so too does the Green Witch, flowing between light and shadow, growth and retreat.

The Twin Moons offer the witch both protection and concealment, empowering them to be seen when needed and to remain hidden when necessary. In this balance lies the secret of Green Witchcraft, a practice rooted in the rhythms of the natural world and the ever-turning cycle of the moon.

Working with the Twin Moons: A Guide

To work with the **Twin Moons** is to align yourself with their energies throughout the lunar cycle. Here are some practical ways to incorporate their power into your magic:

Full Moon Rituals:

- Charge your magical tools by leaving them out under the Full Moon's light.

- Perform spells of manifestation, such as those for love, healing, abundance, and protection.
- Focus on outward growth – start new projects, initiate healing work, and engage with the world around you.

Dark Moon Rituals:

- Cleanse your space and tools with salt or smoke to banish negativity.
- Perform spells of protection, banishing, and shadow work, turning inward for reflection.
- Focus on concealment and shielding – protect your personal energy and intentions, laying the groundwork for future growth.

Lunar Illusion: A Glamour

In the art of Green Witchcraft, Glamour is a subtle and powerful form of magic. It is an illusion – one that shapes how others perceive you, allowing you to control what is seen and what remains hidden. Drawing upon the dual forces of the Twin Moons – the light of the Full Moon and the concealment of the Dark Moon – this spell weaves a veil of light and shadow around you. It enhances the qualities you wish to show and hides the aspects you wish to keep unseen. It is not deception, but a careful crafting of perception, aligning your presence with your will.

Purpose:
To create an illusion that highlights what you want to be seen while concealing or downplaying what you wish to keep hidden. This spell draws upon the energy of both the Full Moon and the Dark Moon to balance visibility and secrecy, creating a subtle and effective glamour.

You Will Need:

- A small silver mirror (to reflect the light of the Full Moon)
- A black cloth (to symbolize the concealment of the New Moon)
- Full Moon water (for radiant light and visibility)
- Dark Moon water (for concealment and shadow)
- Dried lavender (for peace and calm, to maintain balance in the glamour)
- A white candle (for the light of the Full Moon)
- A black candle (for the shadow of the New Moon)
- A quiet, secluded space where you can work with the energies of both moons

Preparation:

Before performing this spell, gather Full Moon water and Dark Moon water. These should be collected during their respective lunar phases, with the Full Moon water blessed under the moon's light and the New Moon water left in darkness to absorb the energy of concealment.

Step 1: Casting the Circle

Begin by preparing your space. Light the white candle to represent the light of the Full Moon, and the black candle to represent the shadow of the Dark Moon. Set the silver mirror and black cloth in front of you, with the two bowls of water nearby. Surround yourself with the dried lavender to bring peace and balance into the spell, ensuring that your glamour is both gentle and controlled.

Stand quietly in the center of your space and close your eyes. Feel the presence of both the Full Moon and the Dark Moon, even if they are not visible. Imagine a circle of light and shadow forming around you, a sacred boundary that will hold and protect your magic.

Step 2: Calling Upon the Twin Moons

First, call upon the power of the Full Moon. Hold the silver mirror in your hands, reflecting the light of the white candle. As you gaze into the mirror, see yourself bathed in the moon's radiance, every feature illuminated. Whisper:

> *"By moon of light, by silver gleam,*
> *I shape the self that others dream.*
> *By light of moon, by glow and grace,*
> *I show the world my chosen face."*

As you speak, imagine the aspects of yourself that you wish to enhance – confidence, beauty, wisdom, calm – coming forward, shining brightly like the moon itself.

Next, call upon the power of the Dark Moon. Take the black cloth and hold it over the mirror, symbolizing the concealment of shadow. Let the darkness fall over the reflection, veiling the parts of yourself you wish to keep hidden. Whisper:

"By moon of dark, by shadow's veil,
I hide the truth, I tell no tale.
By shadow's grace, unseen I stand,
What I reveal is by my hand."

Visualize the qualities or truths you wish to keep hidden becoming concealed, invisible under the cover of the Dark Moon. These might be vulnerabilities, emotions, or secrets – anything you wish to protect from view.

Step 3: Anointing with the Twin Moons' Waters

Now, dip your fingers into the Full Moon water, and gently anoint your forehead, your lips, and your heart. As you do, say:

"By moon's bright light, I show my strength,
I walk with grace, I speak at length.
I shine with radiance, calm and clear,
The light I choose is what they hear."

Feel the water enhancing your ability to project the qualities you wish to be seen, drawing the moon's energy into your presence.

Next, dip your fingers into the Dark Moon water, and anoint your wrists, your throat, and the back of your neck. As you do, say:

"By moon's dark veil, I guard my truth,
Unseen by eye, unknown in proof.
I walk in shadow, safe, concealed,
By my will alone, unrevealed."

As the water touches your skin, feel the quiet power of the Dark Moon cloaking you in protection, concealing that which you do not wish to reveal. This is your hidden strength, the part of you that remains safe from prying eyes.

Step 4: Sealing the Glamour

Take the silver mirror and place it over the black cloth, symbolizing the balance of light and shadow, radiance and concealment. Hold your hands over the mirror and cloth, closing your eyes and whispering:

"By twin moons' grace, this spell I seal,
What I reveal is what they feel.
By light and shadow, day and night,
I shape the truth within their sight."

Let the energy of the Twin Moons – both seen and unseen – settle around you, sealing the glamour you have cast. Know that as you move through the world, you control what is visible and what is hidden, shaping how others perceive you according to your will.

Step 5: Closing the Circle

When you feel the spell is complete, take a deep breath and thank the Twin Moons for their guidance and power. Extinguish the candles, starting with the black candle to release the energy of concealment, and then the white candle to release the energy of light. As you do, say:

"The light shall guide, the dark shall hide,
I walk with both, at my own side."

Charm of the Lunar Veils

The Charm of the Lunar Veils is a subtle, quick spell that requires nothing but your focus, intention, and the power of the Twin Moons – light and shadow. With only an incantation and visualization, you can control what you want others to perceive and what you wish to keep hidden.

Instructions:

Find a Quiet Moment: Take a moment to center yourself, whether standing or sitting. Close your eyes and take a deep breath, drawing your energy inward.
Visualize the Desired Effect:

- If you wish to present a quality, such as confidence or calm, visualize yourself bathed in the radiant light of the Full Moon. Imagine that light enhancing and illuminating what you want others to see.
- If you wish to conceal something, such as anxiety or vulnerability, imagine the dark veil of the Dark Moon falling over that aspect of yourself, shrouding it in shadow and making it unseen.

Recite the Incantation Three Times: As you hold the visualization in your mind, repeat the following incantation three times, with focus and intent:

"By moon of light and moon of shade,
I weave the path that must be made.
What I reveal is what they see,
What I conceal, is known to me."

Release the Energy: As you finish the third repetition, release your visualization and the energy of the spell. Trust that the glamour is now in place, shaping how you are perceived.

Rose Water Glamour Perfume

A Bewitching Aura

This spell calls upon the essence of the rose and the light of the moon, weaving a subtle glamour that enhances the witch's beauty and projects an aura of charm and allure. It is more than a simple perfume – this water carries the essence of enchantment, perfect for any Glamour spell.

You Will Need:

- A bottle of rose water
- A few drops of Full Moon Water
- Fresh rose petals
- A small piece of quartz
- A drop of lavender oil

How to Perform:

1. Into your bottle of rose water, add the rose petals and a small quartz crystal.
2. Add three drops of Full Moon Water, calling upon the moon's radiant light to bless the potion.
3. Anoint the rose water with lavender oil, invoking the calm charm of this sacred herb.
4. Hold the bottle in your hands, close your eyes, and whisper:

   "By moonlight bright and rose's bloom,
   I call to thee, my beauty's tune.
   By scent of rose and charm of night,
   I cast my spell, my beauty's light."

5. Anoint your wrists and neck with the rose water perfume whenever you wish to enhance your aura or project a bewitching glamour. Carry its essence with you, letting the magic unfold.

The Binding of Eternal Beauty

Knot Magic Charm:

In the old ways, knot magic was used to bind and hold. This spell is an ancient charm, meant to lock one's beauty into place. The three cords symbolize the threads of youth, vitality, and life itself, woven into the witch's being through the act of knotting. The power of knot magic binds these qualities, anchoring the witch's beauty to the cycles of nature.

You Will Need:

- Three cords:
  - Yellow for youth, as bright as the summer sun.
  - Green for vitality, fresh as spring's first bloom.
  - Red for blood, deep as life's own river.
- A drop of your blood (for the red cord)
- A strand of your hair (for the green cord)
- An image of yourself (for the yellow cord)

How to Perform:

1. Lay out the yellow cord first. As you tie nine knots, speak:

   "Yellow of sun, as bright as light,
   Youth I bind in this cord tonight."

2. Next, take the green cord. Anoint it with a strand of your hair. As you tie nine knots, speak:

"Green of earth, as fresh as spring,
Vitality I bind, in this cord I sing."

3. Finally, take the red cord. Press a drop of your blood into the cord and tie nine knots, speaking:

   "Red as blood, as life is bound,
   I lock my beauty, in this cord it's found."

4. When all cords are knotted, braid them together, sealing the threads of youth, vitality, and blood into one charm. Keep this braid in a secret place, letting its power grow over time.

Mirror Spell for Amplifying Beauty

This spell harnesses the power of reflection, drawing beauty from the witch's own essence and amplifying it through the magic of the mirror. In the dark stillness, the mirror becomes a portal, reflecting back the charm and radiance the witch wishes to project.

You Will Need:

- A mirror (small, for personal use)
- A pink candle (for love and beauty)
- Fresh rose petals or lavender sprigs
- Full Moon Water

How to Perform:

1. Light the pink candle and place the mirror in front of it. Encircle the mirror with rose petals.
2. Anoint the mirror with Full Moon Water, calling upon the light to enhance your beauty. Recite:

   "By glass and light, reflect and glow,
   My beauty shines, my charm does grow.
   By rose's bloom and moon's soft grace,
   I call my beauty to fill this space."

3. Gaze into the mirror, letting your reflection soften and allow the magic to take hold. See the beauty that radiates from within, and know that it shall project outward.
4. Keep the mirror in a sacred place or carry it with you, using its power to enhance your beauty whenever you choose.

The Magic of Herb Bundles

In the ancient tradition of Green Witchcraft and Traditional Witchcraft, the use of Herb Bundles is one of the most effective ways to harness the natural power of herbs. These bundles – filled with carefully selected herbs and tied with corresponding colors – can be used to attract love, bring luck, call for protection, enhance personal charm, and even invite wealth. Each bundle, when bound with intention and empowered through ritual, serves as a magical tool, amplifying the energy of the herbs and carrying your will into the world.

Herb bundles can be hung in the home, carried on your person, placed on an altar, or used to supplement and bolster other spells. This chapter outlines the creation of five distinct herb bundles, each crafted for a specific purpose and sealed with a ritual incantation to empower and activate its magic when needed.

How to Create and Use Herb Bundles

Each herb bundle is tied with a specific colored bag that corresponds to its magical intention. The herbs placed inside have been chosen for their traditional properties, allowing them to work together to bring about the desired result. Once the bundle is crafted, an intention-setting incantation is spoken over it to imbue it with magical purpose.

Herb Bundles by Purpose

1. Red Bag: Herb Bundle for Attracting Love: This bundle draws love and strengthens emotional bonds. It is ideal for enhancing romance, attracting new love, or nurturing existing relationships.

Herbs:

- Rose petals: For love and beauty.
- Lavender: For peaceful and gentle love.
- Cinnamon: For passion and attraction.
- Basil: For fidelity and commitment.
- Yarrow: To strengthen emotional bonds.

Optional Element: A small piece of rose quartz to amplify loving energies.

2. Green Bag: Herb Bundle for Luck: This bundle is tied to good fortune and success. It brings luck in new ventures, opportunities, and personal goals.

Herbs:

- Basil: To attract luck and positivity.
- Mint: To refresh energy and bring swift luck.
- Clover: A symbol of luck and abundance.
- Chamomile: For prosperity and good fortune.
- Bay leaves: For victory and success.

Optional Element: A lucky coin or a green aventurine crystal for enhanced luck.

3. Purple Bag: Herb Bundle for Wealth: This bundle is for those seeking financial success and prosperity. It draws abundance and opportunity in money matters.

Herbs:

- Cinnamon: For swift financial success.
- Patchouli: To attract wealth and prosperity.

- Basil: For wealth and protection.
- Ginger: For fast success and money flow.
- Alfalfa: To ward off poverty and encourage financial stability.

Optional Element: A small piece of citrine or pyrite to amplify wealth attraction.

4. Black Bag: Herb Bundle for Protection: This bundle creates a powerful barrier against harm and negative energies. It protects the wearer or the space in which it's placed from ill intentions.

Herbs:

- Black salt: For banishing negative energy.
- Garlic: A classic protection herb.
- Sage: For purification and banishing.
- Rue: To protect against curses and the evil eye.
- Rosemary: To strengthen protection and shield against harm.

Optional Element: A piece of obsidian or black tourmaline for additional grounding and protection.

5. Blue Bag: Herb Bundle for Confidence and Charm: This bundle is designed to boost confidence, personal power, and charm, making the wearer more self-assured and magnetic.

Herbs:

- Mint: To refresh the mind and boost confidence.
- Thyme: For courage and inner strength.

- Bay leaves: For confidence and success.
- Cinnamon: For warmth and personal charm.
- Lemon balm: To uplift and enhance charisma.

Optional Element: A carnelian stone to enhance confidence and personal power.

Intention-Setting Incantation:

Once your herb bundle is assembled, you will need to set the intention and imbue the bundle with its magical purpose. This is done by reciting the following incantation three times over the bundle as you focus on the energy you wish to infuse into it.

> *"By herbs of power, bound in might,*
> *I call your purpose, day or night.*
> *By cord and leaf, by will and seed,*
> *I charge you now to meet my need."*
> *"By earth, by fire, by water, by air,*
> *I set this spell with thought and care.*
> *Let love/luck/wealth/protection/confidence rise,*
> *By witch's will and moonlit skies."*
> *"I speak this truth, my will set free,*
> *By this charm, so mote it be."*

After completing the incantation, the herb bundle is charged and ready for use.

How to Activate or Call Upon the Herb Bundles' Power:

To activate the bundle's energy or call upon its imbued purpose, hold it in your hands and repeat the intention-setting incantation again three times. As you chant, visualize the herbs within the bundle releasing their energy and filling you or the space with the desired intention – whether it be love, protection, luck, wealth, or confidence.

How to Use the Herb Bundles:

- Carry the bundle with you to absorb and radiate its energy.
- Hang it in your home to protect, attract, or amplify the specific energy you seek.
- Place it on your altar to enhance your spellwork and connect with the herbs' magical properties.
- Refresh the herbs as needed, and when the spell has fulfilled its purpose, return the herbs to nature by burying them in the earth

The Rites of Seasonal Blessings

This simple ritual will align the witch with the turning of the seasons, calling on the energy of the Full Moon or Dark Moon to bless the land, plants, or a personal intention that corresponds to the current season.

You Will Need:

- A bowl of Full Moon Water or Dark Moon Water (depending on the season)
- Seasonal herbs (like spring flowers, summer leaves, autumn seeds, or winter pine)
- A small silver ribbon (to tie the blessing to the season)

Incantation:

For Spring (Full Moon Water):

"By light of moon, by budding tree,
I call the spring, in growth and glee.
Bless this land, this life, this space,
Let spring's renewal fill this place."

For Summer (Full Moon Water):

"By golden light of moon and sun,
I call on summer's work begun.
Bless this day, this warmth, this life,
Let abundance end all strife."

For Autumn (Dark Moon Water):

> *"By moon unseen, by harvest night,*
> *I call the dark to guard my sight.*
> *Bless this land, this life, this fall,*
> *Let autumn's balance guard us all."*

For Winter (Dark Moon Water):

> *"By quiet moon and silver sky,*
> *I call the dark where shadows lie.*
> *Bless this land, this sleep, this snow,*
> *Let winter's peace in silence grow."*

The Hallow's Eve Rite

A Halloween Ritual to Honor Hecate and the Dark of the Moon

On Samhain night, when the veil between the worlds is at its thinnest, we honor the season of death and the turning of the wheel toward winter. This is a time to celebrate the Dark of the Moon, to offer thanks to the spirits of the dead, and to Hecate, the Guardian of the Crossroads, who watches over the transition between life and death.

This ritual is not about summoning or communicating with the dead, but instead focuses on honoring the season, offering gifts to those who have passed, and celebrating the spooky, mysterious energy of Halloween. In this rite, we give offerings of cakes for the spirits, lighting the path with candles, and thanking Hecate for her protection as we step into the dark half of the year.

You Will Need:

- Small cakes or sweet bread (baked as offerings for the spirits)
- A bottle of red wine (for libation)
- A black candle (to honor Hecate and the Dark Moon)
- A white candle (to light the way for the spirits)
- A bowl of Full Moon Water (for blessing)
- A small bowl of salt (for protection)
- Rosemary incense (for purification)
- Optional: A pumpkin or skull candle holder for a festive, spooky atmosphere

Step 1: Preparing the Space

1. Cleansing with the Witch's Broom: Begin by sweeping the area with your Witch's Broom, clearing away any lingering energies. As you sweep, say:

   "By broom and sweep, I clear this ground,
   No ill may come, no dark be found.
   By salt and smoke, I bless this space,
   A sacred rite, in night's embrace."

2. Lighting the Candles: Place the black candle at the center of your altar to honor Hecate, and light it as you speak:

   "Hecate, Three Crowned Goddess,
   Queen of Night and Shade,
   I honor thee as light doth fade.
   By torch and flame, protect this rite,
   Lend thy Power, lend thy Might,
   Hearken from the Hidden Glade
   The secret road, the Witches' Way,
   I call thee come and guide the path,
   Safe from wicked curse or blast.
   Mistress of the Spirits' Plane,
   Queen of Magic, Queen of Night,
   I honor thee with this rite."

Light the white candle and place it next to the black candle, saying:

"By white flame bright, I light the path,
For spirits passed, both near and far.
On Hallow's Eve, this light shall guide,
I offer peace, no ill shall bide."

Step 2: Offering Cakes and Wine to the Spirits

1. Bless the Cakes and Wine: Lay the cakes on a plate and pour a small glass of red wine. Hold your hands over them and sprinkle a few drops of Full Moon Water over both, blessing them as offerings for the spirits of the dead. Say:

   "By moon's full light and water's grace,
   I bless these gifts for spirits' taste.
   Sweet cakes I give, red wine I share,
   With those who walk beyond the air."

2. Offer the Feast: Place the cakes and wine at the center of the altar, or outside in a place where the spirits may walk. As you do, speak with reverence:

   "Spirits passed, I honor thee,
   By cake and wine, I set you free.
   No ill befall, no shadow near,
   I offer peace, to those held dear."

Step 3: Honoring Hecate and the Dark Moon

1. Call Upon Hecate: Stand before the altar and hold your hands up, calling upon Hecate to bless and protect the ritual. Speak her name with reverence and power:

   "Hecate, Warden of the Night,
   I call upon your ancient might.
   By crossroads dark and moonless sky,
   I honor thee, as night draws nigh."

2. Pour the Libation: Pour a small libation of red wine into the ground or a bowl, offering it to Hecate. As you pour, say:

"To thee, O Queen of Shades and Night,
I pour this wine, as offering right.
By moonless sky and shadow's grace,
I honor thee, O Goddess Great."

Step 4: Celebrating the Season

1. Enjoy the Atmosphere: Take a moment to breathe in the night, listen to the wind, and enjoy the spooky atmosphere of Halloween. Let the dark energy of the season settle around you, knowing you are protected by Hecate.
2. Thanking Hecate: When you are ready to close the ritual, thank Hecate for her protection and presence:

"Hecate, Queen of Night and Shade,
I thank thee for the gift you gave.
By night's dark cloak and flame's soft glow,
I honor thee, and let thee go."

3. Snuff the Black Candle: Gently snuff out the black candle, symbolizing the end of the ritual, and the closing of the dark path.

Step 5: Closing the Circle

1. Closing the Circle: If you have cast a protective circle, now is the time to close it. Walk counterclockwise around the space, saying:

"This rite is done, this circle closed,
No ill may stay, no harm imposed.
By broom and flame, by salt and air,
I end this spell, and leave with care."

2. Leave the Offerings: Leave the cakes and wine outside, in a natural space, to honor the spirits and the season. This simple act completes the offering and connects you to the turning of the seasons.

Charm for Grounding and Centering

This charm is for grounding after intense magical work, bringing the witch back to balance. It calls on the earth's steady energy and can be repeated whenever needed.

You Will Need:

- A small stone or crystal (like hematite or onyx)
- A bowl of water (to wash your hands and ground energy)

Incantation:

"By earth below and sky above,
I ground my heart, I calm my blood.
By stone and soil, my roots go deep,
I call the earth, my peace to keep."

Wash your hands in the water while holding the stone to release the excess energy back to the earth.

Spell of the Hidden Flame

This spell helps reignite passion and motivation when you feel blocked or uninspired. It calls upon both moons to remove blockages and light the inner fire.

You Will Need:

- A candle (red or white, to represent the flame)
- Full Moon Water and Dark Moon Water combined

Incantation:

"By moon of dark, by moon of light,
I call my flame to burn so bright.
By light revealed and shadow cleared,
My passion wakes, no longer feared."

Light the candle, sprinkle the water around it, and visualize your inner fire rekindling.

The Moon's Path Dream Walker

This ritual invites the moon's power into your dreams for guidance or clarity. It enhances dreamwork and divination through sleep.

You Will Need:

- A moonstone or herb pouch with mugwort or lavender (to tuck under your pillow)
- Full Moon Water (for clarity)

Incantation:

"By moonlit path, by dream's soft light,
I walk the realms of shadowed night.
Reveal to me what I must see,
In dream's deep magic, speak to me."

Anoint the moonstone or pouch with the water and place it under your pillow to guide your dreams.

The Binding of the Wayward Spirit

This spell respectfully binds a wayward or disruptive spirit, preventing it from causing harm or interference while allowing it to remain in peace. The binding is focused by attuning to the spirit's presence before the ritual, establishing a direct connection.

You Will Need:

- A black cord or thread (to bind the spirit's energy)
- A pinch of salt (for purification)
- A small personal token related to the spirit (this could be a symbol, object, or something associated with the space the spirit haunts, such as soil or a small stone from the area)
- A black candle (to focus the spirit's energy)
- Dark Moon Water (optional, to anoint the space or object)

Instructions:

1. Attune to the Spirit: Sit quietly in the space where the spirit is most active, or hold the personal token associated with the spirit. Close your eyes and focus on the feeling or presence of the spirit. Visualize the spirit's energy taking form, whether it's a shape, feeling, or presence. As you connect with the spirit, say:

   "Spirit here, I call you near,
   Attend to me; I see you clear."

Imagine the spirit becoming aware of you, and you of it, establishing a respectful connection.

2. Create the Circle with Salt: Pour a circle of salt around the space where you sense the spirit or around the token that represents the spirit's energy. This circle creates a boundary, focusing the binding. As you create the circle, say:

   "By salt of earth, I draw this line,
   To bind your force, this space is mine."

3. Invoke the Binding: Hold the black cord in your hands and begin wrapping it around the token or within the circle of salt. As you do, focus on the spirit's energy being bound by the cord, unable to harm or interfere. Speak the following incantation, repeating it three times:

   "By cord of night, by salt of earth,
   I bind you now, for what it's worth.
   No harm shall come, no ill shall see,
   I bind you here, in peace, let be."

4. Seal with the Candle and Water: Light the black candle to focus the spirit's energy and seal the binding. If you have New Moon Water, sprinkle a few drops on the cord or token, symbolizing the spirit's presence being hidden and bound in peace. As you do, say:

   "By moon unseen and shadow's might,
   I bind your form, out of sight.
   Bound in peace, harm no more,
   locked in space, your power I store."

5. Final Step: Bury the token and cord in the earth or a hidden place to keep the binding strong. This will anchor the spirit to the location without harm. If no physical

token is used, you can symbolically bury the black cord or sprinkle the salt in the space where the spirit resides. As you bury it, say:

"By earth and night, I seal this tie,
Bound in peace, harm no more."

A Healing Spell Invoking the Power of the Twin Moons

This healing spell uses the power of both the Full Moon and Dark Moon to balance health and restore vitality. It can be for the witch or another person.

You Will Need:

- A bowl of combined Full Moon Water and Dark Moon Water
- Healing herbs (like chamomile or thyme)

Incantation:

"By moon of light, by moon of shade,
I heal the wound, I lift the blade.
By full and dark, by peace and rest,
I call the moon to heal what's best."

Sprinkle the herbs in the water and anoint yourself or another with the healing waters.

The Mirror of True Seeing

The Mirror of True Seeing is a powerful artifact in the Green Witch's arsenal. It reflects truth, reveals hidden realities, and wards off Malefica. Once charged under the Full Moon and sealed with water from the Dark Moon, it becomes a permanent tool for protection and divination. It can be positioned in the home to reflect harmful magic and ill intentions back to their source, or it can be used for personal scrying to gain insights into situations, people, or hidden truths.

You Will Need:

- A small mirror (preferably with a silver frame or trim, symbolizing the moon's light)
- Full Moon Water (to charge the mirror with illumination and truth)
- Dark Moon Water (to seal the mirror's protection and concealment)
- A black candle (for scrying and focus)
- A quiet, dark space for the ritual

Charging the Mirror Under the Full Moon

1. Place the Mirror Under the Full Moon: On the night of the Full Moon, set the mirror outside or in a window where it can capture the moon's light. As the light reflects off the mirror's surface, imagine it absorbing the moon's power of illumination and truth. Hold the mirror and say:

"By moon of silver, by moon so bright,
I charge this mirror with your light.

Reflect the truth, reveal what's clear,
By moon's command, make Truth appear."

2. Anoint with Full Moon Water: Gently anoint the mirror with Full Moon Water, sealing the charge. As you anoint, say:

   "By water's grace, this light is bound,
   Reflect the truth, in silver found."

Sealing the Mirror with Dark Moon Water

1. Seal with New Moon Water: On the night of the Dark Moon, place the mirror in a dark room and sprinkle it with Dark Moon Water. This seals the mirror's protective powers, allowing it to guard against Malefica and harmful energies. As you anoint the mirror, say:

   "By shadow's veil, I seal this sight,
   No harm shall come, no ill shall blight.
   By moon unseen and hidden grace,
   This mirror guards its sacred space."

Positioning the Mirror to Reflect Malefica

Once charged and sealed, place the Mirror of True Seeing in a location where it can act as a guardian. The mirror should face outward, reflecting any harmful magic or ill intentions away from your space. It can be placed near a doorway, window, or any area where you feel protection is needed.

Position the Mirror:

As you position the mirror, say:

"By silver light and shadow deep,
This mirror guards, and none shall creep.
By moon's bright face and veil of night,
I send away all harm and blight."

The mirror now acts as a silent guardian, reflecting negative energy away from your home and protecting those within.

Using the Mirror for Scrying

When seeking hidden truths or deeper insights, you can use the Mirror of True Seeing for personal divination. The mirror serves as a portal, allowing you to gaze into the unknown and reveal answers that may be concealed. This ritual should be done in solitude, in a quiet, dark room with only the mirror and a black candle to guide your vision.

1. Prepare the Space: Light the black candle and place it between yourself and the mirror. Sit in a dark room, where there are no distractions, and position the mirror in front of you.
2. Invoke the Moon's Power: Focus on the mirror's surface, allowing your gaze to soften and unfocus. Speak the following incantation:

   "By moon of night, by candle's flame,
   I seek the truth, by secret name.
   Reveal to me what I must know,
   In mirror's depths, the answers show."

3. Gaze into the Mirror: Allow your eyes to drift, staring into the mirror without focusing on any particular point. In the darkness and the candle's flickering light, the mirror becomes a portal, and images or symbols may begin to

form. Trust what you see or sense – whether it's literal images, abstract shapes, or intuitive feelings.

4. Close the Scrying: Once you have finished gazing, extinguish the candle and gently cover the mirror. Say:

"By moon's deep dark and silver gleam,
I close this sight, I end this dream.
What's seen is known, what's felt is true,
The mirror's gaze, I bid adieu."

Covering the mirror helps seal the scrying and close the portal. Use this ritual whenever you seek deeper truths or guidance.

The Boon of Gifts

A Bestowal of Blessing Spell for a Newborn

The Boon of Gifts is a spell meant to bestow blessings upon a newborn child, harnessing the gentle and protective light of the Full Moon. This blessing ensures that the child carries the moon's grace and protection as they grow. The spell involves enchanting a silver coin under the Full Moon, infusing it with light and energy, and then using that coin to bless the child. The coin, once imbued with the moon's power, becomes a protective charm, a quiet guardian hidden beneath the child's crib or bed, watching over them as they sleep.

You Will Need:

- A silver coin (to hold the moon's blessing)
- A bowl of spring water
- A clear night under the Full Moon
- A quiet space for the ritual
- The newborn child (to bless within three days of the enchantment)

Part 1: Enchanting the Silver Coin

1. Prepare Your Space: On the night of the Full Moon, find a secluded place outdoors or near a window where you can see the moon's reflection clearly. Set the bowl of spring water in front of you, ensuring that it can capture the reflection of the Full Moon in its surface.
2. Charging the Coin: Hold the silver coin in your hand, lifting it gently toward the moon. As the light touches the coin, visualize the coin absorbing the moon's radiant

energy, becoming a vessel of grace, peace, and protection. As you focus on this intention, say:

"By moon's bright gleam and silver grace,
I charge this coin, a gift to place.
With light and love, a boon I send,
Upon this child, the moon's own friend."

3. Baptizing the Coin: Lower the coin into the bowl of water, letting it rest at the bottom as the Full Moon's reflection dances across the surface. Let the moon's light fill the water and the coin with its power. As the coin sits in the water, chant softly:

   "By water clear and moon's bright light,
   I bless this coin, this child's right.
   With love to guide and light to shield,
   A boon of blessings now revealed."

Let the coin rest in the water for a few moments, absorbing the moon's reflection and the blessing you have called forth.

Part 2: Bestowing the Boon Upon the Child

Once the coin is enchanted, you have three days to complete the blessing. Find a quiet moment where you can place the blessing upon the newborn, away from distractions.

1. Preparing the Child for the Blessing: Bring the enchanted silver coin and gently hold it in your hand. Hold the coin near the child's head, heart, or simply in the space where the child rests. Close your eyes and focus on the moon's gentle light radiating from the coin.
2. Placing the Blessing: Gently touch the child's forehead with the coin, bestowing the moon's light and your

blessing upon them. As you do so, speak the following words:

"By silver coin and moonlit beam,
I gift this child the brightest dream.
With light to guide and love to keep,
May peace be theirs in wake and sleep."

3. Sealing the Blessing: After placing the coin on the child's forehead, take a moment to feel the energy settling. Visualize the child wrapped in the moon's protective light, surrounded by love and safety.
4. Placing the Coin: Finally, tuck the enchanted silver coin beneath the child's bed or crib, in a place where the child cannot reach it. The coin will act as a constant guardian, carrying the moon's blessing and watching over the child as they grow.

Wild Herb Healing Tonic

For Inner Wellness and Strength

This restorative tonic draws upon the healing power of wild herbs to support your overall well-being. Each herb has been chosen for its medicinal properties, creating a brew that bolsters your vitality and strengthens your spirit.

You Will Need:

- 1 tbsp dried nettle (for strength and vitality)
- 1 tbsp dried elderberry (for immune support)
- 1 tbsp dried peppermint (for digestive health)
- A pinch of dried thyme (for protection and cleansing)
- A pinch of dried lavender (for calm and healing)

Instructions:

1. Boil 2 cups of fresh spring water.
2. Add all the herbs to the boiling water and let steep for 10-15 minutes.
3. Strain the mixture and drink slowly, focusing on the energy of the herbs restoring your body and mind.
4. As you drink, visualize the healing energy flowing through you, promoting strength, health, and well-being.

Incantation:

"By leaf and stem, by root and vine,
Grant me health through nature's line.
Let this brew restore my might,
And keep me well by nature's light."

Incantation for Safety: Mother Moon's Protection

This Incantation for Safety calls upon the protective powers of the Mother Moon, invoking both her light and shadow. It draws upon the five elements - fire, water, earth, air, and spirit - to form a complete shield of protection, uniting the powers of the natural world and the moon's dual forces. The light and dark are bound together in this invocation, providing safety and balance in all spaces.

"By flame and fire, burning bright,
I call your warmth to guard this night.
By water's flow, deep and still,
I call your strength, protect my will.
By earth below, firm and sure,
I call your roots, my path secure.
By air above, swift and free,
I call your winds to shelter me.
By spirit's light and shadow deep,
I call the moon, in wake and sleep.
By Mother Moon, dark and bright,
who watches all that fills that night,
I bind your powers in this light:
Harm me not and disappear; you are vanquished!
Be gone from here!"

Elderflower Beauty Balm

For Radiance and Skin Healing

This soothing balm, made from elderflowers and chamomile, enhances the skin's natural glow and promotes healing. It's perfect for dry, irritated, or inflamed skin and is gentle enough for everyday use.

You Will Need:

- 2 tbsp dried elderflower (for skin rejuvenation)
- 1 tbsp dried chamomile (for calming and soothing)
- ¼ cup beeswax (for moisture and protection)
- ½ cup coconut oil or almond oil (for hydration)
- A few drops of lavender essential oil (optional, for fragrance and healing)

Instructions:

1. In a small pot or double boiler, gently heat the coconut oil and add the dried elderflower and chamomile.
2. Allow the herbs to infuse in the oil over low heat for 30-45 minutes.
3. Strain the oil to remove the herbs, then melt the beeswax into the infused oil.
4. Once fully melted, remove from heat and add a few drops of lavender essential oil if desired.
5. Pour the mixture into a small jar and let it cool.
6. Apply daily to your skin for a radiant, healing effect.

Incantation:

"With flower's bloom and honey's gold,
I heal my skin, smooth and bold.
By nature's grace, my beauty shines,
Radiant glow, this balm is mine."

Protection from Malefica and Evil Spirits

The Green Witch's Shield

This spell creates a powerful shield of protection around you or your home, using the strength of iron, the purity of salt, and the protective energies of rosemary or juniper. It is especially effective against harmful energies or malevolent spirits.

You Will Need:

- 4 iron nails (for strength and protection)
- A handful of salt (for purification)
- A sprig of rosemary or juniper (for warding and protection)
- A small pouch (to contain the items)

Instructions:

1. Place the 4 iron nails, salt, and rosemary or juniper into the small pouch.
2. Hold the pouch in your hands and focus on its purpose of protection.
3. Envision a barrier of light surrounding you or your home, strong and impenetrable.
4. As you visualize this, chant the following incantation with conviction:

   "By earth and iron, salt and vine,
   No evil shall cross this magic line.
   I call the wild to stand with me,
   By nature's power, keep me free and safe from harm."

Once charged, bury the pouch near the entrance of your home or keep it with you as a personal talisman of protection.

The Rite of the Witch's Broom

Crafting and Consecrating Your Sacred Tool

Your witch's broom (besom) is an essential tool for cleansing, protection, and ritual work. This rite will guide you in crafting your own broom and consecrating it for sacred use.

You Will Need:

- A sturdy stick or branch (ash is traditional, but any wood you feel connected to will do)
- Natural fibers or twine for binding
- Dried herbs (such as lavender, rosemary, or sage) for the broom bristles with twigs or corn straw as the lion's share of the broom brush.
- Cleansing incense (for the consecration)

Instructions:

1. Begin by selecting a branch or stick for your broom handle. Ensure that the wood is ethically gathered, either fallen naturally or with permission from the tree.
2. Gather herbs or twigs for the broom's bristles, ensuring they are also collected in harmony with nature.
3. Bind the herbs or twigs to one end of the stick with natural twine or fiber. As you do, focus on the purpose of your broom – whether for protection, cleansing, or ritual work.
4. Once the broom is crafted, light the cleansing incense and pass the broom through the smoke, saying:

"With smoke and air, I cleanse this broom,
With nature's might, I seal its tune.

By herb and wood, this tool shall be,
A guide to cleanse and protect me."

Use your broom to sweep the area where you will perform rituals, always moving clockwise to clear away any negative energy.

Spell to Enchant a Ritual Staff

The Ritual Staff can serve as an alternative to the Witch's Broom in all respects within the spells and rituals of this grimoire. Just as the broom is used to sweep the ritual space and cast the circle, the staff traces the circle, focusing the witch's intent and guiding them through both light and dark. Whether used for protection, casting, or guidance, the enchanted staff stands as a powerful magical tool.

You Will Need:

- A wooden staff (naturally sourced, or one that resonates with you)
- A black candle (for protection and the power of the Dark Moon)
- A white candle (for clarity and the light of the Full Moon)
- A small bowl of salt (for grounding and protection)
- A bowl of Full Moon Water and a bowl of Dark Moon Water (for blessing)
- Optional: Herbs such as rosemary, sage, or mugwort for anointing the staff

Step 1: Preparing the Ritual Space

1. Cleanse the Space: Begin by casting a circle using your current method – whether sweeping with your Witch's Broom or marking the circle with your hands. You are creating a space for transformation, where your staff will be imbued with power.

2. Light the Black and White Candles: Place the black candle on the west side of your space and the white candle on the east. These flames represent the Dark Moon and the Full Moon, the dual aspects of the Twin Moons that will infuse your staff with both light and shadow.

Step 2: Blessing the Staff

1. Anoint the Staff: If you have herbs, gently rub the staff with rosemary, sage, or mugwort to cleanse and prepare it for enchantment. As you do, say:

   "By herb and wood, I cleanse thee whole,
   By moon's soft light, by witch's soul.
   By sage's smoke and rosemary's might,
   Be pure, be blessed, by day and night."

2. Bless with the Full Moon Water: Dip your fingers into the Full Moon Water and sprinkle it over the staff, saying:

   "By moon of light, by water's grace,
   I bless this staff to guard this space.
   By moon full bright and crystal clear,
   I call thee now, protection near."

Then, sprinkle Dark Moon Water over the staff:

"By moon of dark and shadow deep,
I bless this staff, protection keep.
By night unseen, by hidden power,
I call thee now, in darkest hour."

Step 3: Imbuing the Staff with Purpose

1. Trace the Circle: Take the staff and use its end to slowly trace the boundaries of your circle in the ground or air, marking the sacred space. As you do, speak the words of empowerment:

   "By wood and will, this staff I hold,
   Shall mark the line, protect the fold.
   By Twin Moons' light, by earth and sky,
   I cast this circle, none shall lie."

Visualize the circle's edge glowing with a faint light, impenetrable and strong.

2. Invoke Its Power: Now, holding the staff upright, focus your energy and intention into it. Feel the connection between you, the staff, and the Twin Moons. Speak the final enchantment:

   "Staff of mine, by moon and star,
   Guide my path both near and far.
   By night's dark veil and day's bright sun,
   My will is done, the spell is spun."

Step 4: Naming the Staff

To further empower the staff, it must be named, giving it its own identity and role in your magic. The act of naming a tool grants it purpose and allows it to act with greater focus and alignment with your will.

1. Speak the Name Aloud: Holding the staff, think of a name that reflects its purpose and power. Say the name aloud, infusing it with energy as you speak:

   "By name I give, by will I claim,
   [Name], you hold the witch's flame.
   By earth and sky, by sea and tree,
   This name I speak, so mote it be."

2. Feel the Connection: As you say the staff's name, visualize its power aligning with yours. The staff is now a partner in your magical workings, its name binding it to you and your intent.

Step 5: Sealing the Enchantment

1. Seal with Salt: Sprinkle a small circle of salt around the staff where it stands, grounding the enchantment. As you do, say:

   "By salt and earth, I seal this charm,
   Protect my path, keep me from harm."

2. Extinguish the Candles: As you extinguish the black candle, say:

   "By shadow's grace, I thank thee now,
   Protection strong, I take my vow."

As you extinguish the white candle, say:

"By light's soft glow, I honor thee,
By staff and spell, my will is free."

The Rite of the Wand: The Witch's Long Finger

The wand is an extension of the witch's will, the "finger" that directs, commands, and manifests the witch's deepest desires. Aligned with the element of fire, it is a tool of passion and power, most suited to witches whose magic calls forth lightning and whose hearts burn with the desire to manifest. While the wand is not essential to every spell or ritual, it can be a powerful ally when the witch's intent requires focus, direction, or a more tangible way of channeling energy.

The wand is especially useful in spells of manifestation, where the witch's desires are brought forth from the shadowed realm of intention into the light of reality. It also plays a role in the commanding and compelling of spirits, acting as a focal point for authority and control.

This Rite of the Wand calls upon the balancing energies of the Twin Moons – the Full Moon for clarity and light, and the Dark Moon for mystery and shadow. The wand, tempered by fire and consecrated by water, becomes a conduit for both manifestation and control.

The materials of the wand should resonate with the witch's intent and purpose. Here are a few suggested materials:

- Ash: Traditionally used in healing and protection spells. It is a versatile wood that offers strength and balance.
- Rowan: Known as the witch's tree, it is aligned with protection, guidance, and spiritual command.
- Oak: The symbol of endurance, protection, and strength, making it well-suited for powerful workings.
- Hazel: A traditional wood for divination and wisdom, perfect for spells requiring insight and guidance.

The wand is a versatile tool that can supplement other spell work, used to direct energy during incantations, focus the witch's intent, and provide clarity in ritual work. The commanding and compelling of spirits is especially potent when the witch wields a properly consecrated wand, adding both force and authority to their magic.

You Will Need:

- A freshly crafted or ethically sourced wand made from your chosen wood
- Full Moon Water
- Dark Moon Water
- A flame (from a candle or small fire)
- A few drops of anointing oil (optional, depending on intent)
- A small bowl of earth or sand (to represent grounding the tool)

Step 1: Cleansing and Consecrating the Wand with Water

Begin by placing the wand on your altar or within your ritual space. Light a candle to provide a flame for the final step of the consecration. Before invoking the element of fire, the wand must be balanced and purified by the Twin Moons' energies.

1. Anoint with Full Moon Water: Take the bowl of Full Moon Water, representing the light and clarity of the Full Moon, and gently sprinkle it over the wand. As you do, recite:

   "By the light of the moon, I cleanse thee,
   By the power of the night, I bless thee.

Full Moon's radiance, lend your glow,
That this wand's power will ever grow."

2. Anoint with Dark Moon Water: Now, take the bowl of Dark Moon Water, representing the shadows and hidden potential of the Dark Moon. Gently anoint the wand with it, reciting:

   "By the shadow's depth, I cleanse thee,
   By the darkened sky, I bless thee.
   Dark Moon's mystery, lend your might,
   That this wand wields both shadow and light."

Step 2: Tempering the Wand with Fire

After consecrating the wand with the power of the Twin Moons, it must be tempered in flame, as it is an instrument aligned with the element of fire. The flame will not only strengthen the wand but also instill it with the power of manifestation.

1. Hold the wand just above the flame (do not let it touch the fire directly). As you pass the wand over the flame, focus on infusing it with the element of fire, envisioning the flame's energy flowing into the wand, giving it the power to command and manifest.
2. Recite this incantation as you pass the wand over the flame:

   "By flame's bright edge, I temper thee,
   By fire's might, I strengthen thee.
   Wand of wood and flame-born power,
   Manifest my will from this hour."

Step 3: Grounding the Wand

After the wand has been tempered, it must be grounded to balance its fiery energy. Place the wand in the bowl of earth or sand, allowing it to rest there for a few moments. This step grounds the tool, ensuring it remains connected to the natural world and stable for use.

Step 4: Sealing the Ritual

Finally, take a moment to anoint the wand with oil if desired, aligning it with your specific intent – whether for manifestation, commanding spirits, or directing energy. Once the ritual is complete, the wand is now fully consecrated and ready to be used in spellcasting, rituals, or spirit work.

Sealing Incantation:

> *"By light and dark, by flame and earth,*
> *I seal this wand, I give it birth.*
> *Bound to fire and the Twin Moons' grace,*
> *May it serve me in every place."*

Restorative Tea of the Grove

A Potion for Physical and Emotional Balance

This tea restores balance to both body and mind, using calming herbs and ginger for strength and grounding. It is perfect for times when you feel drained or overwhelmed.

You Will Need:

- 1 tbsp dried lemon balm (for calm and clarity)
- 1 tsp dried passionflower (for peace and relaxation)
- 1 tsp dried skullcap (for relieving tension)
- A slice of ginger root (for warmth and grounding)
- Honey (optional, for sweetness and healing)

Instructions:

1. Boil 1 cup of water and add the herbs and ginger to the pot.
2. Let the tea steep for 10 minutes, then strain the herbs.
3. Add honey if desired and sip slowly, allowing yourself to feel the calming energy of the tea spread through your body.

Incantation:

"By leaf and stem, by root and bloom,
Bring me peace, dispel my gloom.
Through nature's heart, I find my way,
In balance now, I'll face the day."

Mirror of the Moon: A Water Scrying Spell

This spell uses Full Moon Water to create a reflective surface through which the witch can gaze into the future or seek answers to important questions. The Full Moon's light enhances the clarity of the vision, while the stillness of the water acts as a mirror to the unseen. The moon's energy helps draw forth visions, while the witch opens their mind to receive the subtle messages hidden in the ripples and reflections.

You Will Need:

- A bowl of Full Moon Water (blessed under the light of the Full Moon)
- A silver coin or small reflective stone (to enhance the reflection)
- A white candle (to create a soft glow)
- A quiet space where you can sit in darkness, preferably near a window with moonlight or outside under the moon

Preparation:

1. Create the Water Mirror: Pour the Full Moon Water into a shallow bowl, creating a still surface. Gently drop the silver coin or reflective stone into the water to help enhance the moon's reflection. Place the bowl in front of you where you can gaze comfortably into it.
2. Light the Candle: Light the white candle and place it beside the bowl, allowing its gentle glow to reflect softly in the water. You want the light to be dim, creating a peaceful, calm atmosphere for divination.

The Spell:

1. Focus Your Intent: Before you begin scrying, take a few moments to clear your mind and focus on your intent. What is it that you seek to know? Whether you're asking for insight into the future or clarity on a decision, form your question clearly in your mind. Then, speak it softly into the water.
2. Invoke the Moon's Guidance: Gently swirl your fingers through the water, stirring it slightly, and say the following incantation:

   "By moon's bright face, by water's glow,
   I seek the truth the night shall show.
   By silver light and scrying's grace,
   Reveal to me, what I must face."

3. Gaze into the Water: As the water stills, fix your gaze on the surface of the water. Allow your mind to relax, opening yourself to any images, symbols, or messages that might appear. The Full Moon's energy will guide you, using the reflections and slight ripples of the water to reveal hidden truths.
4. Receive the Message: Be patient as you gaze into the water. Visions may come as shapes in the reflection, impressions, or intuitive thoughts. Trust what you see or feel – messages may come subtly, but they will carry the weight of the moon's wisdom.

Sealing the Divination:

1. Close the Spell: Once you feel you have received your answer or guidance, gently swirl your fingers in the water again, thanking the moon for its wisdom. As you do, say:

"By moon and water, I thank thee now,
The vision clear, the truth I vow.
What's seen is known, what's felt is right,
I close this scrying, end the night."

2. Extinguish the Candle: Blow out the white candle, sealing the vision and grounding yourself. You may choose to pour the water into the earth as an offering, giving thanks for the moon's guidance.

Green Witch's Hair Gloss

For Lush, Healthy Hair

This natural hair gloss nourishes and conditions your hair, giving it strength and shine. The rosemary promotes healthy growth, while the olive oil and honey moisturize and soften.

You Will Need:

- 2 tbsp olive oil (for moisture and shine)
- 1 tbsp honey (for hydration)
- 1 tbsp apple cider vinegar (for scalp health and shine)
- A sprig of rosemary (for hair growth and strength)

Instructions:

1. Warm the olive oil and honey together in a small pot.
2. Add the apple cider vinegar and rosemary to the mixture.
3. Once warm, apply the gloss to damp hair, massaging it into your scalp and through your strands.
4. Leave it on for 20 minutes, then rinse thoroughly.
5. Use this gloss weekly to maintain healthy, strong hair.

Incantation:

"By rosemary and honey sweet,
I nourish strands from root to feet.
Through nature's gift, my hair will shine,
growing healthy like a vine."

The Enchanted Garden

For the Green Witch, the garden is a place of deep enchantment, where the seen and unseen worlds touch. It is not simply a plot of Earth, but a sacred space where the Green Witch engages with the spirits of the land, the elements, and the magic of life and death. Here, in the quiet spaces between the leaves and under the soil, the witch practices her craft, guided by the rhythms of nature and the cycles of the moon.

The garden is a living grimoire, each plant, stone, and creature carrying within it ancient knowledge and natural power. Through the act of gardening, the witch communes with the earth – learning its secrets, listening to its whispers, and weaving its magic into her spells. As the witch tends the plants, she also tends her own magic, for in the garden, the line between care and spell craft blurs. To plant, to water, to harvest – each is a ritual, a sacred act that nourishes the soul of the land and the witch alike.

Offerings left in the garden – whether they be herbs, milk, or ethically sourced blood – further this bond, feeding the spirits of the soil and ensuring that the earth remains in balance. In return, the land offers its own gifts: bones, feathers, and stones, each imbued with its own magic and purpose, waiting to be discovered and woven into the witch's craft.

The Seedling Charm

This charm is whispered over newly planted seeds to ensure they grow strong under the watch of the Earth spirits and the moon's light.

Incantation for Planting:

> *"By soil and sun, by rain and sky,*
> *I plant thee now, with witch's eye.*
> *By moon's soft glow, by Earth's strong root,*
> *Grow strong, grow wild, bear sacred fruit."*

How to Perform:

As you place the seeds into the earth, speak the incantation. Visualize the life force of the earth surrounding the seed, helping it to root deeply. Sprinkle a few drops of Full Moon Water onto the soil for an added blessing.

Spell to Protect the Witch's Garden

To guard the garden against harm from pests, harsh weather, or negative energies, this spell calls upon the Twin Moons to protect the witch's sacred space.

You Will Need:

- A vial of Full Moon Water
- Rosemary sprigs (for safeguarding)
- A small offering of ethically sourced blood (to nourish the soil)

How to Perform:
Walk the edges of your garden, anointing the soil with a small drop of blood at each corner to nourish the land. As you do, speak this charm:

> *"By root and leaf, I cast this charm,*
> *No ill may come, no pest may harm.*
> *By moon of light and shadow's face,*
> *I guard this garden, I bless this place."*

Then, sprinkle Full Moon Water over the garden, placing rosemary sprigs at each corner to act as wardens.

Growth Enchantment

When plants seem to struggle or falter, the Green Witch may invoke this spell to call upon the sun, moon, and earth to restore their vitality.

You Will Need:

- A small mirror (to reflect sunlight onto the plant)
- A bowl of spring water
- A green cord or ribbon

How to Perform:
Place the mirror near the plant to reflect sunlight onto its leaves. Tie the green cord around the stem or near the base of the plant, then pour the spring water into the soil. As you do, recite:

"By light and root, by rain and sun,
I call thee back, thy strength begun.
By vine and leaf, by soil and air,
Grow strong, grow bright, with witch's care."

Leave the mirror in place for a full day to bathe the plant in the sun's light.

Offering Spell to Nourish the Soil

It is said that the Gods and Spirits of the Earth were the last to cease accepting Human Sacrifice. When your Garden falters, your blood may be the key. This spell is performed to balance and nourish the soil, offering thanks to the earth spirits for their continued growth and protection.

You Will Need:

- A small bowl of milk or honey
- A handful of fresh herbs (such as thyme, basil, or rosemary)
- A small vial of ethically sourced blood

How to Perform:

At dawn or dusk, bury the blood, milk, or honey at the base of a plant in the garden, sprinkling the herbs into the soil. As you perform this act of offering, recite:

> *"By earth and root, by stone and sky,*
> *I offer this with heart and eye.*
> *By herb and blood, by moon and sun,*
> *This garden's spirit now is one."*

As you leave the offering, remain aware of the gifts the land may return – whether in the form of bones, feathers, or stones – each imbued with its own magic.

Spell to Bless and Enchant a Plant or Garden

The Twin Waters of the Moon

This spell calls upon the power of both the Full Moon and the Dark Moon to bless and enchant a plant or garden. By combining the radiant energy of the Full Moon with the shadowed, protective energy of the Dark Moon, the witch infuses the plants with a balance of growth, strength, protection, and vitality. Using Full Moon Water for nurturing and manifestation, and Dark Moon Water for protection and unseen strength, this spell creates harmony in the plants, encouraging them to thrive while remaining guarded from harm.

You Will Need:

- A bowl of Full Moon Water (for growth, illumination, and nurturing)
- A bowl of Dark Moon Water (for protection, strength, and unseen forces)
- A small jar to combine both waters
- Rosemary or lavender (for growth and protection)
- A silver ribbon or thread (to symbolize the moon's blessing)
- A quiet space in your garden or near your plant

Preparation:

1. Prepare the Water: On the night of the Full Moon, leave a bowl of water outside or near a window to absorb the moon's energy. This water will carry the nurturing light of the Full Moon, encouraging the growth and vitality of the plants.

On the night of the Dark Moon, do the same, leaving a bowl of water to gather the protective, hidden energy of the Dark Moon, which will shield the plants from harm and unseen forces.

2. Combine the Waters: On the night you plan to perform the spell, combine equal parts of the Full Moon Water and Dark Moon Water into a small jar, blending the twin energies of light and shadow.

The Spell:

1. Prepare the Garden or Plant: Bring your jar of blended moon water to the plant or garden you wish to bless. Stand quietly for a moment, allowing yourself to connect with the energy of the plants and the earth beneath your feet. If you have rosemary or lavender, you may place a few sprigs near the plant to enhance its energy.
2. Invoke the Full Moon's Blessing: Hold the jar of water in your hands, feeling the Full Moon's energy radiating within. Focus on the plant's growth, health, and vitality, and as you gently pour a portion of the water at the plant's roots, say:

"By light of moon, by silver beam,
I bless this plant, this garden's dream.
In growth and health, in fertile ground,
Let light and life here both be found."

Invoke the New Moon's Protection:

Now, turn your focus to the Dark Moon's energy – the hidden strength that lies in the shadows. Pour the remaining water over the plant's roots, and as you do, imagine the plant being surrounded by an unseen shield of protection. Say:

"By moon unseen, by shadow's might,
I guard this plant from harm and blight.
By roots below and leaves above,
In quiet strength, this plant I love."

Tie the Silver Ribbon:

As a final gesture, take the silver ribbon and gently tie it around the plant or around a stake in the garden to symbolize the moon's lasting blessing. As you tie the ribbon, say:

"By light and dark, by moon's decree,
This plant shall grow, both wild and free.
Protected, strong, beneath the sky,
By moon's twin powers, you shall rise high."

Wildflower Dream Pillow

For Peaceful Sleep and Enhanced Dreaming

A dream pillow filled with calming herbs enhances sleep and encourages vivid, insightful dreams. Place it beneath your pillow to experience its soothing effects.

You Will Need:

- A small muslin or cotton pouch
- Dried lavender (for relaxation and sleep)
- Dried mugwort (for enhanced dreaming)
- Dried rose petals (for love and comfort)
- A small piece of amethyst (optional, for spiritual clarity)

Instructions:

1. Fill the small pouch with lavender, mugwort, and rose petals.
2. If desired, add a small piece of amethyst for dream clarity and spiritual insight.
3. Sew or tie the pouch closed and place it beneath your pillow before sleep.
4. As you settle into bed, repeat the following incantation:

Incantation:

"With lavender, rose, and sacred night,
Guide my dreams with gentle light.
Peaceful rest, now come to me,
Through the wild, my mind flies free."

Incantation to Find a Lost Object

"By shadow's veil and moon's bright glow,
Reveal the path where I must go.
By hidden force and guiding light,
Bring back what's lost into my sight."

Repeat as needed while you search for the sought-after item.

Talisman of the Stag

For Strength, Protection, and Courage

This talisman invokes the powerful spirit of the stag, representing strength, protection, and courage. Wear it during challenging times or keep it near you when seeking bravery.

You Will Need:

- A small bone or antler fragment (ethically sourced, representing the stag's strength)
- A leather cord (for tying the talisman)
- A sprig of oak or pine (for resilience and longevity)
- A red thread (for vitality and protection)

Instructions:

1. Tie the bone or antler fragment to the leather cord using the red thread, infusing the knot with your intention.
2. Braid the sprig of oak or pine into the cord, symbolizing resilience and strength.
3. Hold the talisman in your hands and visualize the protective and courageous spirit of the stag flowing into it.
4. Wear the talisman or keep it close to you when you need strength and courage.

Incantation:

"By bone and wood, by oak and stag,
Grant me strength, where I may lag.
I walk with courage, wild and free,
With nature's power inside of me."

Note of Guidance: A Green Witch's Ethical Practice

As Green Witches, it is our duty to respect the balance of nature. Every spell and ritual in this book is crafted with this core principle in mind: leave no harm upon the earth. When you gather materials, ensure they are collected ethically, without harming the living beings or ecosystems that they come from. Use only biodegradable materials, and never bury items that could damage the environment, such as glass, plastic, or metal.

Green Witches are Wardens of the Wild, protectors of the animals, plants, and sacred spaces that make up our world. By working in harmony with nature, we ensure that our magic heals, strengthens, and nurtures all life.

Shield of Silver, Shield of Night

This incantation, placed at the beginning of your grimoire or stitched into the folds of your Witch's Cloak, calls upon the protective powers of the Twin Moons – the Full Moon's silver light and the Dark Moon's shadowed night. It serves as a magical shield, a blessing of protection to guard you as you work with the forces of the natural world.

"Shield of silver, bright moon's gleam,
Guard my path, protect my dream.
Shield of night, dark moon's veil,
Hide me well where shadows trail.
By light and dark, by moon's twin might,
I walk in peace, both day and night."

Minor Hexes

The Green Witch's Guide to Minor Malefica

In Green Witchcraft, the focus is always on balance and harmony with nature. While we do not seek to harm or curse others, we must acknowledge that Malefica exists in the world, and sometimes justice moves slowly. When we are confronted by malevolent forces or ill intentions, we may need to defend ourselves, protect what we love, or ensure that justice finds its way. These minor hexes are designed not to destroy or harm, but to reflect back the darkness sent to us, to stall the progress of those who would do harm, and to create barriers that guard against further Malefica.

Each of these hexes should be cast with caution and integrity, for Green Witchcraft always seeks to remain aligned with nature's balance. As in all magic, the witch's will and intention are the most powerful forces at work.

The Binding of Harmful Speech

Purpose:

To silence gossip, lies, or harmful words directed toward the witch or their loved ones. The hex ties the tongue of those who speak ill, ensuring their Malefica cannot spread further. Incorporating a Beef Tongue (sourced from a Local Butcher) can heighten the spell as a Ritual Catalyst.

You Will Need:

- A piece of twine or black thread
- A small mirror (for reflecting malice back to its source)
- Dried rosemary (for protection)
- A black candle (for binding)

Instructions:

1. Cast your protective circle with your Witch's Broom, sweeping away any negativity.
2. Light the black candle and hold the mirror up to reflect it, saying:

   "By mirror's face, I now reflect,
   The words of harm, I redirect.
   Malice cast, shall not take flight,
   Bound by mirror, day and night."

3. Tie the twine or thread into three knots, imagining the harmful speech being tied and bound, unable to cause further damage. With each knot, say:

"By knot of one, the tongue is stayed,
By knot of two, the lies will fade,
By knot of three, the harm is sealed,
No voice of malice shall be revealed."

4. Place the rosemary on the mirror to protect against future Malefica, and let the candle burn down.

The Tangling of the Deceiver's Path

Purpose:

To confuse and slow down the actions of someone who seeks to deceive or harm the witch through manipulation or betrayal. This hex causes their plans to falter and their path to be tangled, reflecting the chaos they attempt to sow.

You Will Need:

- A small jar of soil (to represent their path)
- A handful of nettles (for protection and strength)
- A red ribbon (to tangle their actions)
- A thorn from a rose bush (for defense)
- The name of the target on a red slip of paper (or some other personal attachments)

Instructions:

1. Prepare your jar of soil, visualizing the path of the person who seeks to deceive. The soil represents their journey.
2. Add the personal attachment into the jar, repeating the target's name thirteen times.
3. Sprinkle the nettles into the jar for protection, then place the thorn into the soil, imagining it guarding your path from their malice.
4. Wrap the red ribbon around the jar, twisting it in a spiral as you chant:

   "By path of thorns and tangled thread,
   The lies they weave shall now be led,
   To snare and twist, to falter and stall,
   Until their falsehoods break and fall."

5. Seal the jar with wax from the black candle and bury it near a crossroads, symbolizing the hex's power to confuse and divert harmful intentions.

The Withering Glare

Purpose:

This spell is to stall or weaken the influence of a toxic person who seeks to drain the energy and spirit of others.

You Will Need:

- A dried lemon (to represent the withering of their influence)
- A pinch of salt (to purify and preserve your energy)
- A black cloth (to conceal and bind their malice)
- A small piece of obsidian (for protection)
- A picture of the target or some other personal attachment

Instructions:

1. Cut the dried lemon in half, focusing on how this person's toxic energy is draining those around them. Sprinkle salt into the center of the lemon halves to neutralize their influence. Then place the image of the target or other personal attachment in between the lemon halves.
2. Wrap the lemon halves in the black cloth, and tie it shut with a piece of thread (or a knot charm if you'd like to add additional layers of power and influence) as you say:

   "By salt and stone, by cloth of night,
   I cast away their draining blight.
   Withering glare, their power fades,
   No more shall I be bound in shades."

3. Place the obsidian near the bundle to reflect their ill intentions and leave the bundle outside under the waning moon to weaken their influence over time.

The Mirror of Ill-Willed Spirits

Purpose:
To reflect back the ill-will or spiritual Malefica sent your way, ensuring that whatever spirit or force seeks to harm you is turned back upon its sender.

You Will Need:

- A small mirror
- A white candle (for purity and protection)
- Dried lavender and sage (for cleansing)
- A strand of your own hair (to tie the spell to your protection)

Instructions:

1. Light the white candle to create a protective light and burn the sage to cleanse your space.
2. Hold the mirror and sprinkle lavender onto it, saying:

   "By mirror bright, by candle's flame,
   All spirits ill shall turn in shame.
   No harm shall pierce, no curse shall land,
   This mirror shields by my command."

3. Wrap your hair around the mirror's handle or frame, tying the reflection to your personal protection. Leave the mirror where it can reflect the entrance to your home or personal space, ensuring no Malefica can cross the threshold.

The Knotted Malice

Purpose:
To bind and weaken the malicious intent of someone who seeks to undermine or harm you. This hex traps their ill will, holding it at bay and preventing them from further harm.

You Will Need:

- A length of black ribbon (to bind malice)
- An image of the target or another personal attachment (like their name on red paper)
- A sprig of yarrow (for courage and protection)
- A needle or pin (to symbolically pierce their ill intent)
- A black candle (for binding)

Instructions:

1. Knot the black ribbon around the yarrow sprig with the target's personal attachment, focusing on the person who seeks to harm you. Imagine their ill will becoming tangled in the knots, unable to reach you.
2. As you tie each knot, say:

   "By knot of binding, malice stays,
   Your wicked intent shall fade away.
   No harm shall reach my soul, my heart,
   Your malice now is bound apart."

3. Pierce the ribbon with the needle or pin, symbolically halting the flow of their ill will, and hold the ribbon over the flame of the black candle (without burning it) to seal the hex.

4. Keep the knotted charm beneath a protective plant in your garden (or in a black bag in a place with no light).

Hexes in Green Witchcraft

Though these minor hexes may be necessary for self-defense and justice, Green Witchcraft always seeks balance with the natural world. These spells are not crafted for vengeance or harm, but to reflect, protect, and stall the forces of Malefica. Cast with caution and care, these minor hexes can safeguard your path without breaking the harmony that Green Witches strive to maintain.

The Thirteen-Knot Charm

A Spell to Bolster Power and Purpose

This Thirteen-Knot Spell draws on the ancient magic of Witch's Knotwork, focusing on weaving intention into each knot as you tie it. The thick red cord represents willpower and force; each knot binds energy to your desired purpose. This powerful charm can be carried as an amulet for protection, strength, or luck, or it can be used to bolster other spell work. The energy contained within each knot is released slowly over time or in moments of need, making it a versatile and enduring tool in any witch's arsenal.

You Will Need

- A thick red cord (long enough to tie thirteen knots)
- Full Moon Water (for blessing and empowerment)
- A quiet, focused space where you can work undisturbed

The Thirteen-Knot Spell

1. Prepare the Cord: Before beginning the spell, consecrate the red cord by sprinkling it with Full Moon Water, invoking the moon's energy to strengthen your intent. As you prepare the cord, say:

   "By moon of light, by water clear,
   This cord is blessed, the path made clear."

2. Tie the Knots and Recite the Verses: Begin tying the thirteen knots in the cord. As you tie each knot, speak the verse that corresponds to it, focusing your will and intent with each knot you bind.

Verses for the Thirteen Knots:

1. First Knot

   "By this first knot, my will is spun,
   I bind the spell, my work's begun."

2. Second Knot

   "By this second, the power grows,
   My will is strong, as the river flows."

3. Third Knot

   "By this third, my purpose set,
   My will made sure, without regret."

4. Fourth Knot

   "By this fourth, the winds do fly,
   I call their force from earth to sky."

5. Fifth Knot

   "By this fifth, the flame ignites,
   My power grows, both day and night."

6. Sixth Knot

   "By this sixth, the earth stands tall,
   I call its strength, its might, its call."

7. Seventh Knot

"By this seventh, the sea does rise,
I draw its depths, its lows, its highs."

8. Eighth Knot

"By this eighth, the stars do shine,
Their light and strength, forever mine."

9. Ninth Knot

"By this ninth, the shadows flee,
My will is bright, they bow to me."

10. Tenth Knot

"By this tenth, my will takes hold,
Its power shines, both bright and bold."

11. Eleventh Knot

"By this eleventh, the circle's cast,
My spell grows strong, its roots hold fast."

12. Twelfth Knot

"By this twelfth, the power's near,
I seal the spell, my path made clear."

13. Thirteenth Knot

"By this thirteenth, the spell is done,
I bind it strong, my will is one."

Sealing the Cord's Power:

- Once all thirteen knots have been tied, hold the red cord in your hands and focus on the energy now woven into the knots. Visualize the knots pulsing with the strength of your intention, sealed by the verses you've spoken.
- To seal the spell, sprinkle a few more drops of Full Moon Water over the cord and say:

  "By knot of thirteen, my will is bound,
  In this cord, my power found.
  By moon and star, by earth and sea,
  This spell is sealed, so mote it be."

Using the Thirteen-Knot Charm:

1. Carry the Cord as a Charm or Amulet: The cord, now imbued with your intention and strength, can be carried on your person for protection, luck, or guidance. Tuck it into your pocket, bag, or wear it as a charm to keep its energy close to you.
2. Bolstering Other Spellwork: The Thirteen-Knot Cord can also be placed on your altar or tied around other magical tools during spellwork to strengthen or enhance the energy of your rituals. Its bound power will supplement other spells, making them more effective.

The Thirteen-Knot Spell is a timeless and powerful practice in Witch's Knot Magic, allowing the witch to harness energy and will through the act of tying knots. Each knot carries its own verse and intention, creating a concentrated force that can be released when needed. Whether carried as a personal charm or used to boost other spells, this cord serves as a potent magical tool, woven with purpose and bound by will.

Dance and Knot Magic

This ritual allows the witch to capture the winds using Witch's Knot Magic, with the added dynamic of dancing with the Witch's Broom. By tying a red cord, symbolizing willpower and force, around the broom's brush, the witch calls the winds from the four cardinal directions and binds them in knots. This powerful ritual allows the witch to control the winds, gathering them when needed and releasing them at the witch's command.

You Will Need:

- A red cord (to represent willpower and force)
- Your Witch's Broom
- Full Moon Water (for calming and balancing energy)
- Dark Moon Water (for control and hidden power)
- A small bottle or pouch (to contain the winds)
- A white candle and black candle (to represent balance and the power of light and shadow)

Step 1: Preparing the Cord and Broom

1. Prepare the Space: Light the white candle and black candle, placing them on either side of your outdoor space, representing the balance of the Twin Moons. Find a space where the air is free to move and surround it with a circle of salt to ground the energy.
2. Consecrate the Cord and Broom: Sprinkle both the red cord and the brush of the Witch's Broom with Full Moon Water and Dark Moon Water to balance the stillness and

motion of the winds. As you consecrate the cord and broom, say:

"By moon of white and moon of night,
I call the winds to feel my might.
By broom and cord, by will and sky,
The winds shall dance where I do fly."

3. Tie the Cord to the Broom: Tie the red cord firmly around the brush end of the Witch's Broom, preparing it to catch the winds as you move.

Step 2: Catching the Winds

1. Dance with the Broom to Catch the Winds: With your broom, step into the open air and begin to dance, sweeping the broom through the wind as you twirl and move. Feel the wind gathering around the broom as if it's being drawn into the red cord, bound by your willpower.
2. Invoke the Winds by Their Cardinal Directions: As you move, face the East and raise the broom high, sweeping it to catch the wind of Air. Say:

"By wind of East, by Air's first breath,
I call you here, by life and death."

3. Turn to the South, sweeping the broom forcefully to gather the South Wind's heat. Say:

"By wind of South, by flame and heat,
I call your power, rise and meet."

4. Move to the West, letting the broom catch the watery winds of the West, swirling them around you. Say:

   "By wind of West, by wave and sea,
   I call your storm to dance with me."

5. Finally, face North, gathering the cold winds of the North. Say:

   "By wind of North, by earth and stone,
   I call your might, to stand alone."

Step 3: Binding the Winds with Knots

1. Tie the Knots to Bind the Winds: As your dance concludes, stand still and tie four knots in the red cord around the broom. Each knot binds the winds you've caught. For each knot, say:

   "By East I bind your breath of air,
   By South your flame, no force to bear.
   By West your storm, be still and sound,
   By North your cold, I bind you down."

2. Seal the Wind in a Bottle or Pouch: Untie the cord from the broom and place it in a bottle or pouch, sealing the winds within. As you seal the container, say:

   "By broom and cord, the winds are mine,
   I hold them bound by thread and line.
   When time is right, I'll set you free,
   But for now, be still for me."

Step 4: Releasing the Winds

1. Releasing the Winds: When you are ready to release the winds, retrieve the red cord from the bottle or pouch. Untie the knots one by one, facing each cardinal direction as you release the winds. For each knot you untie, say:

   "By East I release your breath of air,
   By South your flame, wild and fair.
   By West your storm, rise from the sea,
   By North your cold, fly wild and free."

2. Final Incantation: As the final knot is undone, raise the cord to the sky, letting the winds carry your intention with them. Say:

   "The winds are free, by knot undone,
   Go forth and fly, my work is done.
   By moon and wind, by thread and might,
   The winds obey, by day and night."

The Rite of the Hollow Moon

A Curse for Banishing Malefica

The Rite of the Hollow Moon is not a gentle spell, but a curse – a spell of dissolution and banishment, meant to break the power of harmful magic and cast it into the shadows of the Dark Moon. This curse draws solely on the concealed energy of the Dark Moon, rejecting and unbinding Malefica, and works best when cast at the height of emotional intensity. With the Witch's Broom to sweep away harmful forces and the Athame to sever their ties, the witch harnesses the tension of their will, amplified by the thrumming incantation that builds with every word.

This spell must be cast with great care and purpose, for it releases dark and potent energy, meant to dissolve malicious forces and send them back into the void from whence they came.

Purpose:

To break and banish harmful magic, curses, or malevolent energy, sending them into the shadows of the Dark Moon where they can no longer do harm.

You Will Need:

- Your Athame (for severing ties to the curse)
- Your Witch's Broom (for sweeping away malefica)
- A black candle (to represent the Dark Moon's power)
- A black bowl (to hold the reflection of the Dark Moon)
- A handful of sea salt (for purification)
- A small mirror (for reflecting and dissolving negative forces)
- A secluded space where you can work under the Dark Moon

Step 1: Prepare the Space

1. Create the Circle with Your Broom: Sweep the area around you with your Witch's Broom, moving counterclockwise to create a sacred space of protection and banishment. As you sweep, say:

   "By broom and dark, I clear this space,
   To cast away all harmful trace.
   No Malefica shall linger here,
   By hollow moon, I cast out fear."

2. Set the Tools: Place the black bowl before you, encircling it with sea salt for purification. Light the black candle beside the bowl, its flame representing the unseen force of the Dark Moon. Set the Athame within reach, as it will be used to sever ties to the curse during the ritual.

Step 2: The Invocation of Malefica

To invoke the power of the Dark Moon and begin the process of banishment, you must first call out and name the harmful force you wish to dispel. Begin by focusing on the Malefica – whether a curse, ill intention, or negative magic – calling it forth with clear intent.

1. Chant the Opening Invocation: Stand before the bowl, and with both hands outstretched over the black flame, chant:

   "By hollow moon and darkened eye,
   I name you here, beneath the sky.
   Bad magic! Come, attend as you are named [insert name/ source of Malefica]"

(Repeat Name three times, then, continue:)
"From shadow born and darkness made,
I call you forth, you are bade! Here, I command,
Inhabit this space!"

(Visualize the Malefica gathering in the focal point of your power, then continue:)

"By the power of the Darkened Moon
I invoke the power of the witches' rune:
North, South, East, and West
Shadows! Bind! And Manifest!
The evil that would harm me here
Is impotent, weak, and full of fear!
Dark Moon's Power! Hecate's Shadowed Face!
What cannot be seen cannot be traced! "

Recite Three Times

2. Focus on the Curse: As you speak these words, imagine the negative energy rising before you, like a black mist coalescing in the air. Feel the intensity building as you continue the chant, each repetition growing louder and more powerful as you call the Malefica into the space.

Step 3: Severing the Ties with the Athame

Once you have called forth the harmful magic, it is time to break its hold. The Athame will sever the ties that bind the curse to you or its victim.

1. Raise the Athame: Hold the Athame high above the black bowl, its blade gleaming in the dim light of the candle.

Focus on the curse, visualizing it as threads or chains that bind you (or the intended target). With a sharp and clear intent, bring the blade down swiftly, cutting through the curse's hold. As you do, say:

"By hollow moon and shadow's edge,
I sever now your evil pledge.
In this dark and hidden hour
By blade and word, I break your power."

2. Feel the Release: As you sever the curse, feel the weight lift, as though the energy is cut away and begins to dissipate. The spell's grip is broken, but it is not yet dissolved.

Step 4: Dissolving the Harm

With the Malefica unbound, you must now dissolve and banish it into the void of the Hollow Moon, never to return.

1. Use the Mirror to Reflect the Harm: Take the small mirror and hold it up to the flame of the black candle, allowing the light to flicker in its reflection. Visualize the Malefica being drawn into the mirror, captured within its reflective surface. Slowly lower the mirror into the black bowl, symbolizing the dissolving of the curse into the shadowed waters. Say:

"I see you now, reflected here,
But in this dark, you disappear.
By hollow moon, your power dies,
Cast into shadow, none shall rise."

2. Dissolving the Malefica: Imagine the curse dissolving in the dark bowl, sinking into the void of the Hollow Moon's unseen energy. The negative force is swallowed by shadow, unable to reform or return.

Step 5: The Final Banishment and Sealing

1. The Final Incantation: With the Malefica dissolved, raise both hands over the bowl and the black candle, feeling the tension of the spell reaching its peak. Recite the final incantation, allowing the words to thrum with power, building in intensity with each line:

   "By hollow moon and darkened light,
   I banish thee into the night.
   No power holds, no spell shall stay,
   Bad magic, begone, be cast away.
   By salt and shadow, deep and pure,
   I cleanse this space, your end is sure.
   Be gone from here, your time is done,
   By hollow moon and witch's power,
   I cast you out – abhorred! Devoured!"

2. Sealing the Spell: Sprinkle the sea salt into the black bowl, sealing the work with purification. As the salt hits the water, imagine it dissolving all lingering remnants of the curse. Use the Athame to draw a counterclockwise circle around the bowl, sealing the banishment. Say:

   "By salt and shadow, by blade and night,
   You (insert target) is broken, gone from sight."

Step 6: Closing the Ritual

1. Extinguish the Candle: Blow out the black candle, sending the last remnants of the malefica into the void of the Hollow Moon. Feel the space grow still and quiet, the tension easing as the spell's energy dissipates.
2. Dispose of the Residual Energy: Carry the black bowl outside and pour its contents into the earth, allowing the dissolved Malefica to return to the ground. If desired, bury the mirror to neutralize any remaining energy.
3. Sweep the Circle Closed: Use your Witch's Broom to sweep the circle counterclockwise, closing the space and clearing any lingering energy. As you sweep, say:

"By broom and night, I sweep away,
The curse is gone, no more to stay." (repeat three times)

The Rite of the Full Moon

A Spell of Supreme Protection

The Rite of the Full Moon is a spell that invokes the supreme protective powers of the Full Moon. Unlike the banishing force of the Rite of the Hollow Moon, this spell draws upon the radiant light of the Full Moon to form an impenetrable shield of protection around the witch or another person they wish to help. The target of this protection need not be present for the ritual; their image or likeness is sufficient to receive the blessing of the Full Moon's guardianship.

This rite is ideal for calling upon the luminous and benevolent energy of the moon to guard the target from harm, Malefica, or ill intent. It mirrors the Hollow Moon Rite in structure, but instead of working with shadow and dissolution, it draws from the bright, manifesting light of the Full Moon.

Purpose:

To invoke the supreme protective powers of the Full Moon, creating a shield of light around the witch or a chosen individual. This protection repels harm, Malefica, and any malevolent forces, ensuring the target's safety and well-being.

You Will Need:

- Your Athame (to direct the Full Moon's protective energy)
- Your Witch's Broom (to sweep away lingering negativity)
- A white candle (to represent the Full Moon's light)
- A silver mirror (to reflect and amplify the moon's energy)
- A bowl of Full Moon water (for purification and protection)

- An image or likeness of the person to be protected (a photograph, drawing, or symbol)
- A secluded space under the Full Moon or near a window where the moon's light can reach

Step 1: Prepare the Space

1. Create the Circle with Your Broom: Use your Witch's Broom to sweep a clockwise circle around your space, clearing away any lingering negativity and preparing the area for protection. As you sweep, say:

   "By broom and light, I clear this space,
   For moon's bright shield, a sacred place.
   No ill shall pass, no harm shall near,
   The Full Moon's guard now gathers here."

2. Set the Tools:
   Place the silver mirror in front of you, positioning it so it can reflect the moonlight. Set the white candle beside the mirror and light it. Position the bowl of Full Moon water in front of the mirror to capture both the candle's flame and the moon's reflection.

Step 2: Summoning the Full Moon's Protection

To call upon the Full Moon's supreme protection, you must invoke its radiant energy and channel it toward yourself or the chosen individual.

1. Focus on the Image or Likeness:
   Hold the image or likeness of the person to be protected in your hands. Visualize the target surrounded by a glowing sphere of pure, silver light. This light pulses

with the energy of the Full Moon, shielding them from all harm.

2. Chant the Invocation:
   Standing before the mirror and the Full Moon's reflection, raise your Athame to the sky and chant the following incantation with purpose and growing intensity:

   "By silver shield and moon so bright,
   I call your guard; I call your light.
   Protect this soul from harm and fear,
   Let no ill thing come ever near.
   By moon's command and starry might,
   Guard them well, both day and night.
   By shield of silver, by moon's decree,
   From harm and shadow, they are free!"

   Feel the energy of the Full Moon building around you, growing stronger with each repetition of the incantation.

Step 3: Charging the Protection with Full Moon Water

1. Anoint the Image or Likeness: Dip your fingers into the bowl of Full Moon water. Gently sprinkle a few drops of the water onto the image or likeness of the person being protected. As you do, say:

   "By moon's bright water, pure and true,
   I seal this shield; I bind it to you.
   No ill may pass, no harm may see,
   By moon's full light, protected be."

2. Seal with the Athame: Hold the Athame over the image, tracing a circle of light in the air around it. This circle is a symbolic barrier that no harm or malevolent force can penetrate. Say:

   "By moon's light, this circle's cast,
   No ill shall enter, none shall last.
   Bound by blade, by moon's true might,
   You are protected, out of sight."

Step 4: Sealing the Spell

1. The Final Incantation: With the image or likeness still before you, hold both hands over the mirror, the candle, and the water. Visualize the protective energy solidifying into a radiant shield around the person, becoming an unbreakable barrier. Recite the final incantation:

   "By moon's bright face and silver gleam,
   I seal this charm, this blessed dream.
   By light of night, and starry grace,
   No harm shall enter this sacred space.
   By moon's decree, by witch's will,
   This shield is cast, and all is still."

2. Close the Circle with the Broom: Use your Witch's Broom to sweep the circle closed, moving counterclockwise this time, sealing the protective spell. As you sweep, say:

   "By broom and light, I close this space,
   The shield is strong, no harm may trace."

Step 5: Maintaining the Protection (optional)

1. Placing the Image: Place the image or likeness of the person being protected in a safe and sacred place – under a pillow, inside a locket, or somewhere meaningful to you or the target. The protection of the Full Moon will remain with them, guarding them from harm.
2. Reinforce the Shield: To maintain the protection, you can reinforce the shield with Full Moon water each month, anointing the image again under the light of the Full Moon to strengthen the spell.

Ritual of Cleansing and Concealment

Rebalancing After Casting Malefica

After invoking minor hexes or engaging with Malefica for the purpose of self-defense, it is vital to cleanse yourself of lingering energies and protect yourself from further intrusion or harm. This ritual taps into the twin energies of the Full Moon and the Dark Moon – the powers of radiant protection and shadowed concealment. The Full Moon blesses the witch with light and visibility, while the Dark Moon offers the power to remain hidden and unseen, shrouded in protective darkness.

This ritual requires water blessed under both the Full Moon and the Dark Moon, symbolizing these dual aspects of nature. The bath will cleanse the witch of any residual Malefica, protect them from harm, and shroud them in protective invisibility, making them unseen to further attacks.

You Will Need:

- A bowl of water blessed under the Full Moon (for radiant protection)
- A bowl of water blessed under the Dark Moon (for enshadowed concealment)
- Dried lavender (for peace and cleansing)
- Dried rosemary (for protection and strength)
- A white candle (to represent the light of the Full Moon)
- A black candle (to represent the dark of the Dark Moon)
- A piece of obsidian or black tourmaline (for grounding and shielding)
- A quiet bathing space (preferably where you can see the sky or feel connected to nature)

Preparation:

1. Gather Water Blessed Under Both Moon Phases: On the night of the Full Moon, leave a bowl of water outside or on a windowsill where it can absorb the moonlight. This water will carry the energy of radiant protection.
   On the night of the Dark Moon, do the same. This water will be charged with the energy of concealment and shadow.
2. Prepare Your Bathing Space: Light the white candle to represent the energy of the Full Moon and the black candle for the Dark Moon. Place the bowl of Full Moon water near the white candle, and the Dark Moon water near the black candle.
   Burn dried lavender and rosemary in a fire-safe bowl or dish to cleanse the space and invite peace and protection.
3. Cast a Circle: Use your Witch's Broom to cast a protective circle around the bathing space, sweeping away any lingering energies. As you do, say:

   "By broom and flame, I cast this space,
   Cleansed of harm, in moon's embrace.
   By twin moons bright and dark of night,
   I now protect, unseen by sight."

Step 1: Drawing Down the Moon's Power:

As you begin the ritual, sit before the **Full Moon water** and hold your hands above it. Close your eyes and visualize the radiant light of the moon bathing you in protective energy. Imagine this light wrapping around you, creating a shield of luminescence that repels any ill will or harm. As you feel this connection, chant:

"By light of moon and water pure,
I cleanse myself, my soul secure.
No malice may cross this line of light,
For I am guarded, day and night."

Step 2: Calling the Shadow's Protection:

Now, move to the Dark Moon water. Hold your hands above it, and focus on the dark, quiet power of the Dark Moon. This is the moon of concealment, of moving unseen through the world. Imagine yourself being enveloped in a cloak of shadow, hidden from Malefica, invisible to those who would harm you. As you connect to this energy, chant:

"By dark of moon and water still,
I walk unseen, as shadows will.
No eye shall see, no ill shall find,
For I am hidden, safe and fine."

Step 3: The Cleansing Bath:

Now it is time to combine the powers of both the Full Moon and the Dark Moon through the sacred act of bathing. Pour both bowls of water – blessed under the Full Moon and the New Moon – into the bath. As you enter the water, imagine the twin energies flowing through you.

First, feel the radiant protection of the Full Moon water washing over you, cleansing away all remnants of the hex or Malefica you have invoked. Let the water purify your body and spirit, clearing away any residual negativity. Then, feel the concealment of the Dark Moon, wrapping you in a cloak of shadow, protecting you from being seen or targeted by further ill will. As you bathe, say:

"By twin moons bright and shadow cast,
I cleanse my soul from spells now passed.
The light protects, the dark conceals,
I walk in balance, harm repels."

Step 4: Sealing the Protection:

Once you have bathed and feel the water's power flowing through you, take the piece of obsidian or black tourmaline and hold it in your hands. This stone will ground you, anchoring the energies of protection and concealment. Hold the stone close to your heart and say:

"By stone of earth, I seal this rite,
Protection strong, both day and night.
No harm shall come, no sight shall see,
I walk in balance, wild and free."

Place the stone on your altar or carry it with you as a talisman of protection and invisibility.

Step 5: Closing the Ritual:

Step out of the bath and thank the energies of the moon for their guidance and protection. Extinguish the candles, starting with the black candle (the concealment of the Dark Moon) and then the white candle (the protection of the Full Moon), saying:

"By twin moons' grace, this rite is done,
Protected, cleansed, my path begun.
By light and dark, I walk unseen,
In balance now, and all between."

Addendum: The Athame's Role in the Ritual

For witches who have consecrated their athame under the Full and Dark Moon, the athame can be used in place of the obsidian or tourmaline during this ritual. The athame, empowered with the dual energies of gathering and protection, serves as a potent talisman for grounding and shielding after invoking Malefica. However, carrying a dagger is not always practical or discreet, especially in everyday life. Stones like obsidian or black tourmaline are smaller and easier to keep with you for continuous protection, making them safer for unobtrusive use.

The choice is yours – whether to use the athame as a symbolic tool in the ritual or to rely on stones for day-to-day protection, the intent and energy remain the same.

Fire Cider and Herbal Potions

In Green Witchcraft, the use of herbal potions is a natural extension of the witch's connection with the earth, drawing upon the power of plants and the elements to heal, protect, and empower. One of the most famous examples of a traditional potion is Fire Cider – an invigorating, immune-boosting tonic made from a blend of spicy and warming herbs. These herbal remedies carry both physical and magical properties, making them potent additions to a witch's repertoire.

Below is a guide on how to make Fire Cider and create your own herbal potions for a variety of magical purposes.

Fire Cider: A Potion for Strength and Vitality

Fire Cider is a spicy, warming potion made with apple cider vinegar, herbs, and spices. Traditionally used to boost the immune system, it also holds magical properties for strength, protection, and invigoration. When you make Fire Cider, you are not only creating a powerful remedy for the body but also a potion infused with fiery energy that can fuel your spells and ward off malefic forces.

You Will Need:

- Apple cider vinegar (base for the potion)
- Horseradish root (for protection and clearing)
- Ginger root (for healing and strength)
- Garlic cloves (for warding off evil and enhancing protection)
- Onion (for spiritual protection and purification)
- Cayenne pepper or hot peppers (for fiery energy and empowerment)
- Honey (for sweetness, healing, and balance)

- Lemon (for clarity and cleansing)
- Optional herbs:
    - Rosemary (for memory and protection)
    - Thyme (for courage and purification)
    - Turmeric (for healing and protection)

Step 1: Preparing the Ingredients

1. Cleanse and Charge the Ingredients: Before chopping your herbs and roots, take a moment to cleanse them with Full Moon Water or simply hold them in your hands, focusing on your intention of strength and protection. Visualize their natural powers awakening as you prepare them.

   "By root and leaf, by fire and sky,
   I call your strength to heal and fly.
   By witch's will and nature's power,
   This tonic grows with every hour."

2. Chop the Herbs and Roots: Finely chop the horseradish, ginger, garlic, onion, and hot peppers. These ingredients not only have physical healing properties but also create a fiery protective barrier against illness and negative forces.

Step 2: Creating the Fire Cider

1. Fill the Jar: Place the chopped herbs and roots into a large, sealable glass jar. You can layer the herbs with care, visualizing them blending their energies

to create a strong, protective potion. Add a pinch of rosemary, thyme, or any other protective herbs you feel connected to.

2. Add the Apple Cider Vinegar: Pour the apple cider vinegar into the jar until all the ingredients are fully submerged. Apple cider vinegar acts as both the base of the potion and a purifying agent, cutting through illness and negativity.
3. Seal the Jar: Seal the jar tightly and give it a good shake to combine the ingredients. Place the jar in a cool, dark space to infuse for at least two weeks. Shake the jar daily, infusing it with your energy and intention for protection, vitality, and strength.

"By fire's heat and vinegar's brew,
This tonic strong shall power renew.
Protection sure, my will made clear,
This potion holds no place for fear."

Step 3: Straining and Using the Fire Cider

1. Strain the Mixture: After two to four weeks of infusion, strain the liquid through a fine mesh or cheesecloth into a clean jar. The resulting Fire Cider is now charged and ready for use. Add honey to taste, balancing the fiery heat with sweetness, symbolizing balance in your life.
2. Use as a Tonic: Drink 1-2 tablespoons of Fire Cider daily to boost your immune system, especially during cold and flu season. Spiritually, each sip offers protection from malefic forces and strengthens your personal energy.
3. In Spellwork: Fire Cider can also be used in magical workings. For protection spells, sprinkle a few drops around your home or onto your altar. For strength,

drink a dose before a ritual, charging your energy. For empowerment, use it to anoint protective charms or amulets.

Herbal Potions for Magical Purposes

In addition to Fire Cider, you can craft other **herbal potions** to enhance your magic. These potions can be consumed, used in anointing rituals, or sprinkled around your sacred space to invoke specific energies.

Potion for Peace and Calm

This herbal potion brings tranquility, emotional healing, and mental clarity, perfect for calming stressful situations or promoting restful sleep.

You Will Need:

- Lavender flowers (for peace and relaxation)
- Chamomile flowers (for emotional healing)
- Lemon balm (for calming the mind)
- Mint leaves (for clarity)
- Honey (for sweetness and balance)

How to Make:

1. Steep the lavender, chamomile, lemon balm, and mint in hot water for 5-10 minutes.
2. Strain the herbs and add a teaspoon of honey to sweeten the potion.
3. Drink this potion before bed or during moments of stress to invoke calm and inner peace.

"By leaf and flower, calm takes root,
My mind is clear, all stress is mute.

By peace of earth and water's flow,
I drink this brew, and calm shall grow."

Protection Potion for the Home

This potion is designed to protect your home from negative energies, malefic spirits, and ill-intentioned individuals. It can be sprinkled around your home or used to anoint doorways and windowsills.

You Will Need:

- Rosemary (for protection)
- Sage (for purification)
- Bay leaves (for warding off evil)
- Full Moon Water (for blessing)

How to Make:

1. Steep the rosemary, sage, and bay leaves in boiling water for 10 minutes, then strain.
2. Add Full Moon Water to the potion.
3. Sprinkle the potion around the perimeter of your home or anoint windowsills and doorways, repeating:

"By leaf and moon, this house I bless,
No ill may enter, no curse may press.
By herb and light, protection's near,
This home is safe, no harm is here."

Healing Potion for Strength and Renewal

This potion is made with herbs that support physical healing, strength, and energy renewal, perfect for those recovering from illness or needing a boost in vitality.

You Will Need:

- Ginger root (for strength and warmth)
- Turmeric root (for healing)
- Elderberries (for immunity)
- Honey (for sweetness and balance)

How to Make:

1. Simmer the ginger, turmeric, and elderberries in water for 15 minutes.
2. Strain the liquid and sweeten with honey.
3. Drink this potion during times of weakness or fatigue, calling upon the herbs for strength.

"By root and berry, strength returns,
My body healed, my spirit burns.
By herb and honey, warm and strong,
I drink this brew, my life made long."

Herbal Remedy for Protection

Herbs for Protection:

- Rosemary: Used for strong protective energy and purification.
- Sage: Known for warding off evil spirits and cleansing spaces.
- Thyme: Offers strength and protection in magical workings.
- Black Pepper: A powerful herb for banishing and guarding against negativity.
- Bay leaves: A symbol of victory and protection.

Remedy: Protective Herb Pouch

Create a protective charm by combining these herbs in a small black or white pouch. You can carry it with you or hang it in your home for continuous protection.

You Will Need:

- Dried rosemary (for protection)
- Dried sage (for purification)
- Bay leaf (for guarding against harm)
- Pinch of black pepper (for banishing negative forces)
- Small black or white cloth pouch

How to Make It:

1. Combine all the dried herbs in a bowl, focusing on your intention of protection.
2. Place the herb mixture into the pouch, tying it closed with a string.
3. As you tie it, repeat:

   "By herb and leaf, I call protection,
   This charm will ward from ill intention.
   No harm may cross this line I set,
   By earth and will, this spell is met."

Herbal Remedy for Love and Attraction

Herbs for Love and Attraction:

- Rose petals: Symbolizing love, romance, and emotional healing.
- Lavender: For calm, peace, and emotional balance in relationships.

- Basil: Promotes fidelity and passionate love.
- Cinnamon: Used to enhance attraction and warmth in love.
- Yarrow: Strengthens emotional bonds.

Remedy: Love-Attracting Tea

This **herbal tea** blends herbs traditionally associated with love and attraction. Drink it to draw love into your life or enhance self-love.

You Will Need:

- Dried rose petals (for love)
- Dried lavender (for peace in relationships)
- A pinch of cinnamon (for warmth and attraction)
- Dried basil (for passion)
- Honey (to sweeten love and add balance)

How to Make It:

1. Brew the rose petals, lavender, basil, and cinnamon in hot water.
2. Let the tea steep for 5-10 minutes, focusing on your intention to draw love and emotional connection.
3. Strain and add a spoonful of honey, stirring clockwise while reciting:

   "By flower, leaf, and spice so sweet,
   I call love's power, true hearts shall meet.
   By honey's warmth and passion's flame,
   Love shall grow, by magic's name."

4. Drink this tea when performing love spells or when you seek to enhance self-love and emotional well-being.

Herbal Remedy for Healing and Strength

Herbs for Healing:

- Chamomile: Soothes anxiety and promotes restful sleep.
- Elderberries: Boosts the immune system and wards off illness.
- Peppermint: Helps with headaches, digestion, and mental clarity.
- Ginger: Known for warming the body, promoting circulation, and fighting colds.
- Turmeric: A powerful anti-inflammatory and healer.

Remedy: Healing Herbal Elixir

This **healing potion** is designed to support physical recovery, boost immunity, and bring warmth to the body during times of illness or weakness.

You Will Need:

- 1 tbsp dried chamomile flowers (for calming and healing)
- 1 tbsp dried elderberries (for immune support)
- 1 tsp dried peppermint (for clarity and digestion)
- 1 tsp fresh ginger root (for warming and healing)
- 1/2 tsp turmeric (for inflammation and strength)
- 1-2 tsp honey (for sweetness and balance)

How to Make It:

1. Boil water and add the chamomile, elderberries, peppermint, ginger, and turmeric.
2. Let the mixture simmer for 10-15 minutes, then strain.
3. Add honey to sweeten and bring balance.
4. Stir while focusing on healing energy and say:

"By herb and root, by flower and leaf,
I call upon the balm of relief.
By fire's warmth and earth's pure might,
I drink this brew, my strength alight."

5. Drink this potion when feeling run down, or when you need to restore your energy and vitality.

Herbal Remedy for Abundance and Prosperity

Herbs for Abundance:

- Basil: Known for its ability to attract wealth and success.
- Cinnamon: Used to speed up financial success and increase abundance.
- Mint: Invites fresh energy and prosperity.
- Chamomile: Attracts luck, wealth, and good fortune.
- Bay leaves: Symbolizes success, victory, and achievement.

Remedy: Abundance-Attracting Sachet

This sachet is filled with herbs that draw prosperity and success. Keep it near your workspace, wallet, or on your altar to attract abundance.

You Will Need:

- Dried **basil** (for attracting wealth)
- Dried **mint** (for fresh energy and new opportunities)
- Dried **chamomile** (for good luck and fortune)
- **Cinnamon stick** (for speeding up success)
- **Bay leaf** (for victory and success)
- A small **green cloth pouch**

How to Make It:

1. Combine all the herbs and the cinnamon stick in the green pouch.
2. Hold the pouch in your hands, focusing on your intention of prosperity. Say:

   "By herb and leaf, I call success,
   By magic's power, wealth shall bless.
   By mint and bay, by cinnamon sweet,
   Abundance flows to where I meet."

3. Carry the pouch with you, or place it in your wallet or workspace to draw in prosperity and abundance.

Herbal Remedy for Cleansing and Purification

Herbs for Cleansing:

- Sage: Purifies the space and clears away negative energy.
- Lemon balm: Uplifts the spirit and cleanses the mind.
- Lavender: Cleanses and soothes the energy of a space.
- Rosemary: Wards off harmful energies and brings clarity.
- Juniper berries: Used to protect and purify sacred spaces.

Remedy: Cleansing Herbal Bath

This herbal bath is designed to cleanse your energy, purify your spirit, and refresh your mind after stress or difficult times.

You Will Need:

- Dried sage (for cleansing)
- Dried lavender (for calming and purification)

- Dried lemon balm (for clarity and uplifting energy)
- Dried rosemary (for warding off negativity)
- A handful of juniper berries (for protection and purification)

How to Make It:

1. Steep the herbs in a pot of hot water for 10-15 minutes.
2. Strain the herbal water and add it to your bathwater.
3. As you soak in the bath, focus on releasing all negativity and say:

   "By leaf and herb, I cleanse my soul,
   By water pure, I am made whole.
   By sage and flower, this spell I weave,
   All ill departs, I am relieved."

4. Relax in the bath, letting the herbs cleanse your energy and restore your spirit.

Working with Fire Cider and Herbal Potions

Incorporating Fire Cider and herbal potions into your magical practice connects you directly to the natural world and the healing powers of the earth. Whether you're creating a potion for protection, healing, or peace, these concoctions merge physical and spiritual healing into one. As you work with these potions, remember to honor the plants and elements, knowing that their energy flows into every brew you make, enhancing both your health and your magic.

Witch's Flying Ointment

Mugwort's Dreaming Path

In the practices of Traditional Witchcraft, the flying ointment has long been a tool to open the gates of the otherworld, guiding the witch into realms where spirits dwell and visions are clear. Rooted in the belief that certain herbs hold the power to induce trance states and spirit flight, flying ointments are whispered through folklore as gateways to altered consciousness. Whether seeking a path through dreaming, astral travel, or visionary work, the witch who wields this ointment calls upon ancient forces to carry them beyond the veil.

Mugwort, a sacred herb in the craft, is often at the heart of these ointments, known for its potent ability to heighten psychic vision and aid in dreamwork. Blended with other herbs of power, the flying ointment serves as the witch's compass in the unseen realms. However, with this power comes a great need for caution, for the herbs used can be strong and should be handled with care.

This recipe offers both the traditional formula and safer alternatives, for the modern witch who seeks to explore the boundaries of spirit flight without undue risk.

You Will Need:

- 1 tablespoon of Mugwort (*Artemisia vulgaris*)
- 1 teaspoon of Dittany of Crete (for spirit manifestation)
- 1 teaspoon of Wormwood (for visions; optional)
- 1 teaspoon of Yarrow (for protection during spiritual travel)
- A base of organic fat (such as lard or coconut oil) as the ointment carrier

- A few drops of essential oil (optional: lavender for calm, sandalwood for grounding)

While rooted in traditional witchcraft practices, this Flying Ointment recipe includes herbs like Mugwort, Wormwood, and Dittany of Crete, which all have potent effects and must be handled carefully. Here's a breakdown of the safety concerns associated with the herbs mentioned:

1. Mugwort (Artemisia vulgaris): This herb is commonly used in dream work and is generally considered safe in small amounts. However, it can cause allergic reactions in some people, especially those allergic to ragweed or other plants in the Asteraceae family. Mugwort should not be ingested in large quantities, and it is not recommended for pregnant or breastfeeding individuals as it can stimulate uterine contractions.
2. Wormwood (Artemisia Absinthium): Wormwood contains thujone, a compound known for its psychoactive properties. While it is used in some traditional witchcraft practices, it can be toxic in large doses and may cause seizures, hallucinations, or other severe side effects if not handled properly. Topical use of wormwood (as in an ointment) is considered safer than ingestion, but it should still be used cautiously, and prolonged use should be avoided.
3. Dittany of Crete (Origanum Dictamnus): This herb is used in esoteric practices and is considered safe in small amounts. It is often used for protection and spirit manifestation. While there are few reported adverse effects, it's still wise to test for any potential allergic reactions before applying.
4. Yarrow (Achillea Millefolium): This herb is typically safe for external use. However, some people may experience

skin sensitivity or allergic reactions, particularly if they have allergies to ragweed or related plants.

5. Base and Essential Oils: Coconut oil or lard is generally safe for most skin types. Essential oils, while potent, can be safe when used in proper dilution (typically 1-2%). Be cautious of any potential skin sensitivities or allergies.

Precautions:

- Topical Use Only: This ointment should never be ingested, as some of the ingredients, especially wormwood, can be toxic when consumed internally.
- Patch Test: Before using the ointment on a larger area, patch test a small section of skin to ensure you don't have an allergic reaction.
- Consultation: If you have pre-existing health conditions or are pregnant/breastfeeding, avoid the use of herbs like Mugwort and Wormwood. Consult with a healthcare provider or a trained herbalist before using these herbs.
- Small Quantities: Use only in small amounts and sparingly – a little goes a long way. The intent of a flying ointment is not to overwhelm the senses but to subtly guide the mind into altered states of consciousness.
- Protection and Grounding: Always ensure that you ground yourself after using the ointment for any form of spirit work or astral travel.

If you are looking for a milder alternative, consider leaving out or reducing the Wormwood, or substituting it with a less intense herb like lavender to create a safer, gentler ointment for dream work.

Safer Substitutions:

- Lavender can be used in place of Wormwood for a gentler effect. Lavender soothes the mind and helps with relaxation and dreamwork.
- If you wish to avoid using Wormwood altogether (due to its potent thujone content), substitute with Rosemary or Bay Leaf, both of which are known to aid in clarity and psychic protection without the harsher properties of Wormwood.

Step 1: Preparing the Herbs

Begin by grinding together the Mugwort, Dittany of Crete, Wormwood (or its substitute), and Yarrow. As you grind the herbs, speak your intention aloud. Mugwort will be your guide, drawing you into the dreaming world, while Yarrow serves as your protector during the journey. Dittany of Crete, known for its power to manifest spirits, ensures your passage is safe and clear.

Step 2: Infusing the Ointment

Melt the organic fat over a low flame. Once melted, slowly stir in the ground herbs. Let them simmer gently for 20 minutes, stirring occasionally as the fat absorbs the essence of the herbs. As you stir, envision the veil between worlds thinning, allowing you to pass freely.

After 20 minutes, strain the herbs from the ointment base, and let the fat cool. As it begins to solidify, the ointment is ready to hold its magical purpose.

Step 3: Enchanting the Ointment

Hold the ointment in your hands, focusing on your intent. This ointment is a bridge between the realms, aiding you in astral travel or vision work. Recite the following incantation as you charge the ointment:

"By Mugwort's dream and Wormwood's sight,
I call the spirits of the night.
Yarrow guards, and Dittany shows,
The way to where the spirit goes.
By this balm, I take to flight,
And walk the path beyond the night."

Your Flying Ointment is now enchanted and ready for use.

Step 4: Using the Flying Ointment

Apply the Flying Ointment sparingly to your temples, wrists, or soles of the feet before entering a trance, meditation, or ritual. The ointment is designed to guide you into dream states, visions, or spirit flight, where the boundaries of the seen and unseen blur.

As you enter a space of deep meditation or spirit journeying, focus on the slow rising and falling of your breath, allowing the ointment's magic to gently lead you into the otherworld.

Caution:

- This ointment is intended for external use only. Avoid ingesting it.
- If using Wormwood, be aware of its potent effects and consider patch-testing the ointment on a small area of skin before full use.
- For those wishing a milder experience, substitute Lavender or Rosemary for a gentler yet still potent guide through the dreaming realms.

Poppets and Sympathetic Magic

In the world of traditional witchcraft, the use of poppets and Sympathetic Magic is one of the most ancient and powerful practices. Sympathetic Magic works on the principle that "like affects like," meaning that by influencing an object that represents a person, place, or situation, you can influence the actual subject in the material world. In the case of a poppet, this doll becomes a stand-in for the person you wish to affect – whether for healing, protection, banishment, or blessing.

What is a Poppet?

A poppet is a small, handmade figure, usually made from natural materials such as cloth, herbs, sticks, or wax, and imbued with a connection to the person it represents. This connection is created by incorporating something personal, such as:

- A strand of hair
- A piece of clothing
- A photograph
- A written name or signature

Once crafted and connected, the poppet acts as a magical conduit, allowing the witch to influence the person through the actions performed on the doll.

How Sympathetic Magic Works

Sympathetic Magic is based on the belief that a connection exists between the symbolic object (in this case, the poppet) and the person it represents. This allows the witch to direct their energy and intention toward the person by working with the poppet. Actions performed on the poppet – whether to heal, protect, or bless – are reflected in the person's life.

In this magical system, the relationship between the witch, the object, and the person is sacred and powerful. The energy you pour into the poppet transfers to the person it represents, aligning their physical and spiritual state with your intention.

Common Uses of Poppets in Sympathetic Magic

Poppets can be used for a variety of purposes, and the intention behind their use is what drives the magic. Some of the most common applications include:

- Healing: Using the poppet to channel healing energy toward someone who is ill or in need of emotional restoration. Herbs like rosemary, lavender, or chamomile can be used to amplify the healing process.
- Protection: Creating a poppet to ward off harm and protect the person from negative forces or influences. The poppet can be empowered with protective herbs like sage, black pepper, or salt.
- Banishment: When a relationship or harmful influence needs to be removed, the poppet can be used to symbolically banish the person from your life or space. This is often done by casting the poppet away or burying it far from the home.
- Blessing: Poppets can be submerged in a ritual bath or placed on an altar to bless the person with love, peace, or success. This is especially effective when using herbs and moon water to channel positive energy.

The Ethics of Sympathetic Magic

Although poppets are powerful tools, their use requires careful thought and intention. Sympathetic Magic should always be used responsibly, with respect for the person you are influencing. In Green Witchcraft, the focus is on working in harmony with natural forces and using magic for good purposes – such as healing, protection, or peaceful resolution. It's important to approach poppet magic with clarity of mind and purity of intent, ensuring that the energy you send into the world is positive and just.

The Rite of the Poppet

Crafting a Doll for Influence Through Sympathetic Magic

The Rite of the Poppet calls upon the ancient principles of Sympathetic Magic, in which a representation of a person – such as a poppet or doll – becomes a conduit to influence that individual. By binding this poppet to someone using a physical or symbolic connection, you can direct your will to heal, banish, or guide them toward compromise. This spell draws deeply from traditional witchcraft practices, using natural materials to craft the poppet and calling upon the Twin Moons to empower your intent.

You Will Need:

- Natural materials to craft the poppet (cloth, twine, sticks, or herbs)
- A connection to the person (hair, personal item, handwriting, or photo)
- A needle and thread (for binding the doll to the person)
- A small pouch for herbs, stones, or other symbolic materials to amplify your intent
- Full Moon Water and Dark Moon Water
- A black or white candle, depending on the purpose
- Optional: Healing herbs (for healing), banishing herbs (for banishment), or calming herbs (for compromise)

Step 1: Crafting the Poppet

1. Gather Materials: Use natural materials to form the poppet. You can shape it from sticks, sew it from cloth,

or weave it from herbs. The important part is that this poppet acts as a physical representation of the person you wish to influence.

2. Bind the Connection: As you craft the poppet, sew or attach a personal connection to the person. This could be a lock of their hair, a small personal item, a piece of their handwriting, or a photograph. Bind this item into the poppet using thread to establish the sympathetic connection. As you bind the item, chant:

"By thread and tie, by twine and spell,
This doll becomes where you now dwell.
By blood, by hair, by written hand,
You are bound to this my command."

Step 2: Empowering the Poppet with Sympathetic Magic

1. Consecrate the Poppet with Moon Water: Once the poppet is fully crafted and bound to the person, sprinkle it with both Full Moon Water and Dark Moon Water, invoking the balance of light and shadow. Say:

"By moon of white and moon of black,
I call your power, none shall lack.
This poppet holds the truth within,
By moon and will, my work begins."

2. Position the Poppet: Place the poppet before you with the candle (either black for banishing or white for healing/ compromise) positioned beside it. Light the candle, visualizing the flame representing your influence over the person. Focus your intent – whether to heal, banish, or bring compromise – and see the person's energy aligning with your will.

Step 3: Setting Your Intentions

For Healing:

1. Use Healing Herbs or Stones: Place healing herbs (like rosemary, thyme, or chamomile) inside a small pouch and tie it around the poppet's neck or near its heart. Visualize the person receiving the energy of restoration and renewal.
2. Chant for Healing:

   "By moon of light and healing's way,
   I call upon this gentle ray.
   Restore the strength, return the soul,
   By earth and sky, make them whole."

3. Complete the Healing: Leave the poppet in a peaceful place where it will not be disturbed, letting it absorb the healing energy over time.

For Banishment:

1. Use Banishing Herbs or Stones: Add banishing herbs (like black pepper, garlic, or sage) to a pouch and tie it around the poppet. Focus on cutting ties with the person, removing their influence from your life.
2. Chant for Banishment:

   "By moon of night and shadow deep,
   I send you far, away you keep.
   No harm shall cross, no words shall stay,
   By moon and flame, be gone this day."

3. Complete the Banishment: Once the banishment is complete, bury the poppet in the earth or dispose of it far from your home to finalize the severance.

For Compromise:

1. Use Calming Herbs or Stones: Place calming herbs (like lavender, mint, or rose petals) into a pouch and tie it around the poppet. Visualize the person being softened, open to dialogue and understanding. Chant:

   "By moon of shadow and moon of light,
   I draw your heart to what is right.
   Speak with peace, and come to me,
   By moon and will, let us agree."

Keep the poppet close to you during any discussions or confrontations with the person, reinforcing the sympathetic bond until you have reached an understanding.

The Spell of Benevolent Submersion

A Healing and Blessing Rite

This spell works through Sympathetic Magic to bring healing, blessing, and protection to the person represented by the poppet. The doll, acting as a conduit, is submerged in a bath of Full Moon Water and carefully selected herbs that promote healing, peace, and vitality. As the poppet soaks in the blessed water, the witch recites a powerful chant to invoke the moon's light and the earth's natural forces to bring goodness to the target of the spell. This is a spell of pure intention, only used for beneficial influence.

You Will Need:

- A poppet or doll (crafted using sympathetic magic with a personal connection to the person, like hair, a photo, handwriting, etc.)
- A large bowl or cauldron filled with Full Moon Water
- Herbs for healing and protection (such as rosemary, lavender, chamomile, and mint)
- A white candle (for invoking the moon's protective light)
- Optional: Crystals like rose quartz or clear quartz for additional healing energy

Step 1: Preparing the Bath of Full Moon Water

1. Create the Bath: Fill a large bowl or cauldron with Full Moon Water, which has absorbed the energy of the moon for healing and blessing. The water should be still and reflective, ready to receive the doll.

2. Add Healing Herbs: Gently sprinkle the chosen herbs into the water, visualizing their healing properties infusing the liquid. For example:

- Rosemary for strength and vitality
- Lavender for peace and calm
- Chamomile for healing
- Mint for clarity and rejuvenation

As you add each herb, say:

"By leaf and flower, by stem and root,
I call your power to take deep root.
In water's flow, your strength will steep,
Bless this soul in healing deep."

Step 2: Submerging the Poppet

1. Place the Poppet in the Bath: Gently place the poppet into the bath, ensuring it is fully submerged in the Full Moon Water and surrounded by the healing herbs. This act represents immersing the person in the healing and protective energy of the spell.
2. Light the White Candle: Light the white candle beside the bath to represent the Full Moon's protective light. Focus on the person's well-being, visualizing them being wrapped in a soft, radiant glow that heals, calms, and blesses them.

Step 3: Chanting the Healing Incantation

1. Chant the Spell for Blessing and Healing: Stand over the bath, focusing on the person and their connection to the

doll. Feel the energy of the moonlight, herbs, and water working in harmony. Begin chanting the incantation, letting the words flow with intention and magic:

"By moon of white and water pure,
I bless this soul, their healing sure.
By herbs that steep and water's grace,
I call upon the moon's embrace.
Wash away all hurt and fear,
Bring peace and light, draw blessings near.
By witch's will, by moon's bright light,
I cast this spell for love and might."

2. Continue Chanting: Repeat the incantation as the poppet rests in the bath, allowing the water and herbs to work their magic. The doll, bound by Sympathetic Magic, absorbs the healing energy, which is then transferred to the person it represents.

Step 4: Letting the Spell Steep

1. Let the Poppet Steep: Allow the doll to remain submerged in the water for a few minutes, soaking in the combined energy of the Full Moon Water and the herbs. As it steeps, focus on the intention of healing and protection.
2. Conclude the Spell: Once you feel the poppet has absorbed enough energy, carefully remove it from the water. Hold it in your hands and say:

"This work is done, this blessing cast,
May health and peace forever last.

By moon, by water, by witch's hand,
I bless your path, your soul, your land."

3. Dry the Poppet: Gently dry the poppet, and either keep it in a safe, sacred space or give it to the person if appropriate, knowing the healing energy will continue to flow to them.

Addendum: Using Poppets to Strengthen Spells and Rituals

Poppets can be a powerful addition to other spells, rituals, and incantations, working as a physical and magical extension of your intent. When combined with other forms of magic, a poppet acts as a symbolic anchor, amplifying the effects of the spell by creating a direct link to the person or situation you wish to influence. By incorporating poppets into your broader magical practices, you can strengthen the energy of your workings and focus the flow of intention with greater precision.

How Poppets Supplement Other Spells

1. Amplifying Healing Spells: When casting a spell for healing, a poppet can be used to enhance the focus and direction of the energy. By incorporating the poppet into a healing ritual, you allow the energy of the spell to flow directly into the poppet, which in turn channels it toward the person. For example:

    Submerge the poppet in Full Moon Water during a healing bath ritual, as the moonlight's energy strengthens the person's recovery.

Place healing herbs or stones inside the poppet before chanting a healing incantation.

2. Enhancing Protection Rituals: Poppets can be added to protection spells to make the protective energy more personal and specific. By binding a poppet to the person you want to protect, you create a focused point for the protective energy. You might:

   Craft a poppet, surround it with protective herbs and symbols, and place it on your altar while performing a protection circle.

   Anoint the poppet with New Moon Water or salt, and speak an incantation to guard the person against harm.

3. Strengthening Banishing Spells: When you need to remove a harmful influence, a poppet can help banish negativity by acting as the representation of the unwanted force. Integrating a poppet into a banishing spell ensures that your intent to remove the person or influence is sharply focused. You could:

   Bind the poppet with black thread while casting a banishing spell, and bury it away from your home to symbolize the removal of negativity.

   Use the poppet alongside an exorcism ritual to expel a harmful entity or influence, ensuring that both the spirit and its connection to the person are broken.

4. Supporting Compromise and Reconciliation: For spells meant to encourage peace or reconciliation, poppets provide a tangible link to the person you are trying to reach. Placing the poppet near your working area during

a compromise ritual can strengthen your connection with the person, softening their energy. You might:

Wrap the poppet in calming herbs and sprinkle it with Full Moon Water while reciting an incantation for peace.

Use the poppet as a focus during discussions, visualizing a peaceful resolution while it rests nearby.

Layering Magic with Poppets

By layering the use of poppets with other magical workings, you enhance the overall power of the spell. The poppet serves as a bridge between the physical and spiritual aspects of the ritual, allowing the energy to focus and build momentum. Whether used in healing, banishing, protection, or reconciliation spells, the poppet deepens the connection between the witch and the desired outcome. For example:

- Combine a poppet with a candle spell, placing it beside the candle to let the flame's energy charge the poppet.
- Use poppets to focus the energy during an incantation or ritual, visualizing the person receiving the full power of the spell.

Communing with the Spirits of Nature

In Green Witchcraft, living in harmony with nature is not only a central philosophy but also a powerful form of magic. This spell is designed to help the witch align with the natural rhythms and energies of the earth, fostering a deep connection with the land, plants, animals, and elements. By practicing this spell regularly, the witch invites balance, harmony, and mutual respect with nature, allowing them to live in peace with the wild and harness its energies for magic.

You Will Need:

- Green candle (symbolizing nature, growth, and harmony)
- A small bowl of spring water
- Freshly gathered herbs, flowers, or leaves from your local environment (foraged ethically, respecting the land)
- A stone or crystal found in nature (such as quartz, moss agate, or any stone that calls to you)
- Full Moon Water for anointing
- Optional: Feathers or other natural items found in your walks through nature

Step 1: Preparing the Space

1. Find a Sacred Space in Nature: This spell is best performed outdoors in a natural setting, such as a forest, garden, or any place where you feel connected to the earth. If performing the spell indoors, gather elements from nature (such as stones, herbs, or flowers) to create an altar space that connects you to the natural world.

2. Light the Green Candle: Light a green candle, symbolizing the vibrant energy of nature and the harmony you seek with the land, plants, and animals around you. As you light the candle, focus on the flame and visualize yourself becoming one with the environment.

   "By fire's glow and earth's embrace,
   I seek to live in nature's grace.
   By green and flame, I call to thee,
   In nature's heart, I am free."

Step 2: Gathering Nature's Offerings

1. Offer Gratitude to Nature: Hold the bowl of spring water in your hands, and take a moment to offer gratitude to the natural world. Speak your thanks to the earth, air, water, and fire – the elements that support life. Visualize the water carrying your gratitude into the earth.

   "To earth and sky, to leaf and stone,
   I offer thanks for all you've grown.
   By wind and wave, by fire and tree,
   I thank you now and leave you be."

2. Gather Herbs, Flowers, or Leaves: Gently gather a few herbs, flowers, or leaves from your surroundings, foraged with respect and care. As you collect each plant, ask for permission and leave a small offering of water or simply your thanks.

   "By nature's grace, I gather here,
   With love and care, my heart sincere.

By leaf and root, by flower and tree,
I honor you, and you honor me."

Step 3: Connecting with the Earth

1. Sit and Ground Yourself: Sit quietly on the ground or in your sacred space, holding the stone or crystal you found in nature. Let your body sink into the earth, feeling the support of the land beneath you. Close your eyes and take several deep breaths, connecting to the heartbeat of the earth. Imagine your breath becoming one with the wind, your heartbeat aligning with the pulse of the earth, and your spirit merging with the life around you.
2. Anoint the Stone or Crystal: Dip your fingers in the Full Moon Water and anoint the stone or crystal you hold. As you do, visualize the stone as a symbol of your connection to nature and the harmony you seek. Let it absorb the water, the moon's energy, and your intention.

"By moon and stone, by earth and air,
I honor nature, strong and fair.
By water's flow and fire's might,
I seek to live in nature's light."

Step 4: The Incantation for Harmony with Nature

As you sit with the stone, herbs, and candle, speak this incantation to align your spirit with the forces of nature. Visualize yourself as a part of the natural world, fully integrated with the earth's cycles.

"By leaf and branch, by root and seed,
I call the earth to meet my need.

By wind and sky, by rain and fire,
I call to being, my heart's desire."

Step 5: Sealing the Spell

1. Sprinkle the Water: Take the remaining spring water and sprinkle it gently around your space, offering it to the earth and the elements. As you sprinkle the water, imagine it bringing balance and peace to the land and your relationship with it.
2. Extinguish the Candle: Gently extinguish the green candle, sealing the intention of your spell. Allow the flame's energy to linger, knowing that the connection you've made with nature will continue to grow and strengthen.

Maintaining the Harmony

1. Return the Herbs to Nature: After the ritual, return the herbs and flowers you gathered back to nature. Bury them in the earth or scatter them in a meaningful place, symbolizing your ongoing respect for the natural world.
2. Carry the Stone or Crystal: Keep the stone or crystal with you as a reminder of your connection to nature. It can be placed on your altar or carried with you to continue aligning with the spirit of the wild.

Walking in Harmony with Nature

This spell strengthens your relationship with the earth, helping you live in harmony with the natural world and attune to its rhythms. In Green Witchcraft, the bond between the witch and nature is sacred. By nurturing this connection through ritual and intention, you not only protect the natural world but also empower your own magic. As you walk in harmony with nature, your spells will grow stronger, more grounded, and aligned with the flow of life around you.

The Eggshell Protection Charm

This simplified charm draws on the protective qualities of ground eggshells – a symbol of boundaries, purity, and protection – combined with the cyclical power of the Full and New Moon. Stored discreetly under the bed, this charm acts as a ward against harm or ill-intentioned energies while you sleep. The charm must be tended to once a month by anointing it with water blessed under the Full Moon and the New Moon, ensuring that the protection remains balanced and strong.

You Will Need:

- Ground eggshells (for protection and boundary setting)
- A small red pouch (for strength and warding)
- A small bowl of water blessed under the Full Moon
- A small bowl of water blessed under the Dark Moon
- A drop of lavender essential oil (optional, for peace and rest)
- A quiet space to perform the charm's monthly tending ritual

Creating the Eggshell Protection Charm:

1. Preparing the Eggshells: Gather clean, dried eggshells and grind them into a fine powder using a mortar and pestle. As you grind the eggshells, focus on their protective qualities, imagining them creating a safe and secure boundary around you as you sleep.
2. Filling the Pouch: Once the eggshells are ground, fill the red pouch with the powder. As you do, say:

"By shell of earth, by ward of red,
Protect my heart, protect my bed.
No ill shall pass, no harm shall see,
This charm protects and shelters me."

3. Adding the Final Touch: (Optional) Add a single drop of lavender essential oil to the pouch to promote peace and restful sleep alongside protection. Close the pouch tightly, visualizing it sealing away any negative energy that seeks to enter your space.
4. Placing the Charm: Place the pouch under your bed, near the center, where it will remain as a constant ward against harm. The protective energy of the eggshells will form an unseen boundary, guarding you while you sleep.

Monthly Tending Ritual:

Once a month, during the lunar cycle, the charm must be anointed with water blessed under the Full Moon (for radiant protection) and water blessed under the Dark Moon (for concealment and safety in shadow). This ensures that the charm remains strong and balanced, constantly refreshed by the twin energies of the moon.

Instructions for Anointing:

During the Full Moon: Place the pouch in front of you, and dip your fingers into the Full Moon water. Gently anoint the pouch with a few drops, focusing on the protective light of the moon filling the charm. As you anoint, say:

"By light of moon, I bless this charm,
Protect and guard from every harm."

During the New Moon: Repeat the process with the Dark Moon water, this time focusing on the energy of concealment and protection through darkness. Gently anoint the pouch with a few drops, saying:

> *"By shadow's grace, I seal this charm,*
> *Unseen, unheard, from those who harm."*

The Rite of Lunar Exorcism

Banishing Malefic Spirits with the Authority of Hecate

This spell calls upon the supreme authority of Hecate, crowned by the phases of the Twin Moons. Hecate, the Warden of the Night, guards and guides the witch in both the spiritual and physical realms with her Twin Torches, which burn away devils and malevolent spirits. This rite uses both Full Moon Water and Dark Moon Water to dispel and banish malefic spirits from a person or space, consecrating the space and sealing it with the power of the Most High One.

You Will Need:

- A black candle and a white candle (to represent Hecate's Twin Torches and the Twin Moons)
- Your Witch's Broom (to cast the circle)
- Your Athame (for severing the spirit's ties)
- A bowl of Full Moon Water and Dark Moon Water
- Four small bowls of salt (for the cardinal directions: North, South, East, and West)
- An image or object tied to the haunted person or place (if applicable)

Step 1: Casting the Circle and Consecrating the Space

1. Prepare the Space: Place a bowl of salt at each of the four cardinal directions: North (Earth), South (Fire), East (Air), and West (Water). Light the black candle and white candle, representing the balance of the Twin Moons and Hecate's Twin Torches. Place the Full Moon Water and Dark Moon Water between the candles.

2. Cast the Circle with the Witch's Broom: Using your Witch's Broom, sweep the space in a clockwise direction to cast the circle and consecrate the area for the ritual. As you sweep, visualize the space being cleared of negativity. Say:

   "By broom and moon, I cast this ring,
   Hecate's torches guard all things.
   By salt and fire, by air and sea,
   This space is sacred, blessed and free."

3. Consecrate the Space with Moon Water: Sprinkle the Full Moon Water around the circle first, then follow with Dark Moon Water, consecrating the space with the balance of light and shadow. Say:

   "By water of light and water of night,
   I bless this space with Hecate's might.
   No harm shall cross, no evil stay,
   This place is sealed, both night and day."

Step 2: Invoking the Power of Hecate and the Twin Moons

Invoke Hecate's Authority: Raise your Athame and visualize Hecate standing at the crossroads, crowned by the Twin Moons and holding her Twin Torches. Call upon her authority to guide and empower the spell. Say:

"Hecate, crowned by moons of twin,
Warden of night, let this begin.
By torch of black and torch of white,
I call your power, protect this night."

Call Upon the Twin Moons: Pour Full Moon Water over the object or image of the haunted person or space to reveal the spirit, and follow with Dark Moon Water to bind and dispel it. Chant:

"By moon of white and moon of black,
I call the force to drive you back.
By Hecate's torches, burning bright,
Reveal the harm, then fade from sight."

Step 3: Banishing the Spirit

1. Sever the Spirit's Ties: Hold the Athame over the haunted space or person, visualizing the Twin Torches burning away the spirit's hold. With a sharp motion, sever the ties, empowered by Hecate's authority. Speak with strength:

   "By Hecate's blade and torches bright,
   I sever the ties that bind your night.
   By moon's command, by fire's glow,
   I cast you out, you must go."

2. Expel the Spirit with the Twin Moons' Power: Sprinkle the combined Full Moon Water and Dark Moon Water across the area, visualizing the spirit dissolving into shadow, banished by the light and dark forces of the Twin Moons. Say:

   "By moon of shadow, moon of light,
   I send you far from mortal sight.
   Hecate's flame consumes your power,
   Be gone from here, this sacred hour."

Step 4: Sealing with Hecate's Flame

1. Seal the Space with Salt: Walk the perimeter of the circle, sprinkling salt from the bowls at the cardinal points to seal the space and purify it. As you do, speak clearly:

   "By salt of earth, this place is sealed,
   By torch and moon, all harm revealed.
   No shadow shall cross, no devil's might,
   This space is bound by flame and light."

2. Invoke Hecate's Continued Protection: Blow out the black candle, imagining Hecate's torch of shadow still burning. Blow out the white candle, visualizing her torch of light still glowing with protection. As you crown her with the Twin Moons, say:

   "Hecate crowned by moon of light,
   Hecate crowned by moon of night.
   By torch and fire, by moon and star,
   Your power guards, both near and far."

Step 5: Closing the Circle

1. Close the Circle: Sweep the circle counterclockwise with your Witch's Broom, closing and grounding the energy. As you do, say:

   "By broom and blade, I close this space,
   The work is done, all harm erased.
   By Hecate's power, by moon's embrace,
   This circle's closed, I leave no trace."

Dream-Shield Abjuration

This spell calls upon the protective light of the Full Moon to banish nightmares and create a shield of peace around you as you sleep. The Silver Dreamshield ensures restful sleep, free from fear, by surrounding the sleeper in the Full Moon's radiant glow. Nightmares are dispelled, replaced with gentle dreams, while the moonlight guards against any ill-intended spirits or energies that may attempt to intrude during the night.

You Will Need:

- A white candle (to represent the Full Moon's light)
- A silver thread or ribbon (to symbolize the moon's protective shield)
- A bowl of Full Moon water (for purification)
- Lavender or rosemary (for peace and restful sleep)

Instructions:

1. Prepare the Space: Light the white candle beside your bed or in your sleeping space, allowing the flame to represent the protective light of the Full Moon. Sprinkle the lavender or rosemary around the bowl of Full Moon water, inviting peaceful and calm energies into the space.
2. Invoke the Full Moon's Protection: Take the silver thread and gently wrap it around your hand, visualizing it as the moon's light forming a shield around you. Hold the thread over the candle's flame without burning it, letting the light empower the thread with protection. As you focus, say:

"By moon of silver, moon of light,
I banish fear, I guard this night.
No shadow shall cross, no ill shall creep,
Your light protects, in peaceful sleep."

3. Anoint with Full Moon Water: Dip your fingers into the Full Moon water and gently anoint your forehead and heart, sealing the protective energies within. Say:

"By water's grace and moon's pure glow,
I cast out fear, no harm shall show.
My dreams are safe, no nightmares rise,
Beneath your light, all shadows die."

4. Create the Dreamshield: Tie the silver thread loosely around your wrist or place it under your pillow. This thread will continue to protect you as you sleep, ensuring the nightmares are banished and peace reigns in your dreams.
5. Final Incantation: Stand before the candle and, as you extinguish it, speak the final words:

"By silver shield, I sleep in peace,
From moon to dawn, my mind's release.
By moon's command, I rest secure,
No harm shall touch, my dreams are pure."

The Nightmare's Shadow

The Nightmare's Shadow is a minor hex that calls upon the Dark Moon's power to send conjured nightmares upon a target. These nightmares are glamours and figments, illusions woven from the shadows of the moon, designed to unsettle and disturb their rest. Though frightening, they are not true devils or monsters, but manifestations of the Dark Moon's energy, meant to unsettle but not physically harm.

You Will Need:

- A black candle (to represent the Dark Moon's power)
- A small black mirror (to reflect the conjured nightmares)
- A piece of dark fabric (to hold the nightmare's intent)
- A few drops of Dark Moon water (for shadowed energy)
- An image or symbol of the target (a photograph, name, or drawing)

Instructions:

1. Prepare the Space: Light the black candle, its flame flickering faintly in the darkness, representing the hidden and shadowed power of the Dark Moon. Place the black mirror in front of you, reflecting the candlelight in the shadows. Set the dark fabric beside the mirror and sprinkle a few drops of Dark Moon Water onto it, charging it with the moon's energy.
2. Focus on the Target: Hold the image or symbol of your target and visualize them in their sleep. Imagine shadows creeping into their dreams, conjured by the New Moon, weaving themselves into unsettling visions and figments. As you focus, chant:

"By moon of night, by shadow's veil,
I conjure fear, I send this tale.
By figment false, by glamour's might,
Your sleep is plagued, your dreams take flight."

3. Project the Nightmares: Hold the black mirror in front of the candle flame, reflecting both the light and the darkness. Imagine the nightmares forming within the reflection – figures from the shadows, illusions created by the moon's dark energy. Dip your fingers into the Dark Moon Water and anoint the image of the target, saying:

"By moon unseen, by shadow's breath,
I send these dreams, I conjure death.
Not real, but false, in shadowed fright,
Your dreams are cursed, this Hollow Night."

4. Bind the Intent with the Dark Fabric: Place the image or symbol of the target inside the dark fabric, folding it into the cloth. As you wrap it, imagine the nightmares sinking into the target's mind. Speak the final words of the hex, building intensity with each line:

"By moonless night, by shadow's hand,
Your dreams are bound by my command.
In figment dark and shadow's curse,
These nightmares come, no dream reversed."

5. Conclude the Hex: Extinguish the black candle, letting the darkness consume the light, sealing the nightmare in place. Keep the dark fabric hidden in a secret place until the hex's effects have run their course.

The Feast of the Spirits

A Ritual to Commune with the Dead Under the Dark Moon, in the Name of Hecate

On the night of the Dark Moon, when the world is cloaked in darkness, the witch steps between the worlds, calling upon Hecate, the Guardian of the Dead and Queen of Witches. The dead walk again through her power, and their voices may be heard. This night is sacred, a time to honor the spirits and receive their wisdom, guided and protected by Hecate's twin torches.

This ritual includes a feast of baked rosemary bread and red wine, blessed with Full Moon Water to open the path to the spirits. Hecate, crowned by the Twin Moons, watches over the witch and the dead alike, keeping the ritual safe as the veil thins.

You Will Need:

- Baked rosemary bread (a traditional offering to the spirits)
- A small goblet of red wine (to offer alongside the bread)
- A bowl of Full Moon Water (to bless the offerings)
- A black candle (representing Hecate and the New Moon)
- A small dish of salt (for protection)
- Optional: Photographs or mementos of deceased loved ones or spirits you wish to contact
- A plate for the offering
- Rosemary or mugwort incense (to purify the space)

Step 1: Preparing the Sacred Space

1. Cleansing the Circle with the Witch's Broom: Begin by sweeping your ritual space with your Witch's Broom,

moving counterclockwise to banish all unwanted energies. As you sweep, speak with rhythm and purpose:

"By broom, by hand, I clear this way,
No ill may come, no harm may stay.
By air and smoke, by flame and night,
I cleanse this space for sacred rite."

2. Light the Black Candle: Place the black candle at the center of your space, surrounded by a ring of salt. Light the candle and say:

"Hecate, Queen of Witches, hear,
I light this flame, your path draws near.
By night's dark veil and torch of might,
Protect this rite, O Queen of Night."

Step 2: Consecrating the Feast of the Spirits

1. Blessing the Bread and Wine: Place the rosemary bread and red wine on the plate. Drip a few drops of Full Moon Water over the bread and into the wine, consecrating them as offerings for Hecate and the spirits. Speak with intention:

"By moon's bright eye and water's grace,
I bless this feast, I bless this place.
By bread and vine, by grain and grape,
The spirits come, the dead awake."

2. Call Upon Hecate: Lift your hands above the offerings, calling upon Hecate to guide the spirits to your circle. Say:

"Hecate, Queen of Night and Grave,
By your light, the path I pave.
By bread and wine, this feast I lay,
Come guard this night, and lead the way."

Step 3: Opening the Veil to the Dead

1. Summoning the Spirits: If you seek to commune with specific spirits, place their mementos near the offering. Close your eyes and feel the veil thin as you call the spirits with a rhythmic chant:

   "By moonless night and Hecate's grace,
   I call the dead to this sacred place.
   Come forth, ye souls, both kind and wise,
   Walk with me now beneath dark skies."

2. Offering the Feast: Lift the plate of bread and wine as an offering to Hecate and the spirits. Speak with a steady beat:

   "This bread I give, this wine I share,
   For those who walked beyond the air.
   By wine's red blood, by bread of Earth,
   I honor death, I honor birth."

Step 4: Communion with the Spirits

1. Listening to the Spirits: Sit quietly, feeling the presence of the spirits gather around the feast. Hecate watches over, ensuring that only those spirits who offer wisdom and

guidance may come forth. Let your senses open to their presence – whether through whispers, visions, or a deep knowing.

2. Ask for Guidance: If you wish to ask the spirits for guidance, speak your question aloud or in your heart. Allow the spirits to answer in their own time and way.

Step 5: Closing the Rite

1. Thanking Hecate and the Spirits: When you are ready to close the ritual, thank Hecate and the spirits for their presence. Speak with reverence and rhythm:

   "Hecate, Queen of Crossroads and Fate,
   I thank you now, I close the gate.
   By bread and wine, by flame and night,
   I honor thee, O Queen of Light."

2. Dismissing the Spirits: Release the spirits back to their rest, saying:

   "Spirits who walked in shadow's fold,
   I thank you now, your tales are told.
   Return to night, return to sleep,
   I send you back, to darkness deep."

3. Snuff the Candle: Gently snuff out the black candle, symbolizing the closing of the path between the worlds. As you do, say:

   "By flame I close, by night I seal,
   This spell is done, this bond is real."

Step 6: The Final Offering

Leave the Feast for Hecate and the Spirits: To complete the ritual, take the plate of bread and wine and leave it at a crossroads, by a tree, or another sacred place associated with Hecate. As you leave the offering, say:

> *"By Earth and Night, this feast I give,*
> *To Hecate, and those who live*
> *Beyond the veil, beyond the sky,*
> *I leave this gift, and now goodbye."*

The Rite of the Spirit Speaker

The Rite of the Spirit Speaker is a powerful spell, enabling the witch to call upon the spirit of a deceased loved one through the Magic Mirror, allowing for guidance, comfort, and protection. However, beyond communion, this spell grants the witch the ability to craft a permanent amulet from the personal item of the deceased, ensuring the spirit's continued presence as a guardian. A powerful tool in all witchery, this amulet allows the spirit to shield the witch wherever they go, extending the protection and bond beyond the ritual itself.

A Reliquary Pendant with a personal attachment of the deceased – be it hair, a photograph, or a beloved keepsake – is an excellent catalyst for crafting this powerful amulet, binding the spirit to the witch in times of need.

You Will Need:

- A Magic Mirror (previously enchanted under the Twin Moons)
- A black candle (to symbolize the veil between the worlds)
- A bowl of Dark Moon Water (to summon the spirit)
- A personal item of the deceased loved one (photograph, jewelry, letter, or hair)
- A strand of your own hair or a drop of blood to bind the connection
- A Reliquary Pendant or a suitable amulet to house the spirit

Step 1: Casting the Circle of Protection

Begin by casting a protective circle, using your Witch's Broom or Ritual Staff to sweep and cleanse the space. The circle creates a sanctuary where the spirit can safely enter and where you are shielded from harmful forces. Recite:

"Circle of the Whitest Moon,
Imbue in thee, a holy boon.
Protection around, a spirit within,
Shield me from harm, guard me from sin."

Step 2: Summoning the Spirit through the Magic Mirror

Place the Magic Mirror on your altar, ensuring the black candle is reflected in its surface. Place the personal item of the deceased near the mirror. This item acts as a tether, drawing the spirit closer.

Hold a strand of your hair or drop of blood and drop it into the Dark Moon Water, linking you to the spirit. As you gaze into the mirror, speak the following incantation:

"Through shadowed veil, by moon's dark grace,
I summon thee to this sacred place.
Spirit sister, mother, friend, or kin,
Come forth now, as I call you in."

Gaze into the mirror and allow your vision to blur. Sit in silence, giving the spirit time to articulate itself. Be patient, as the spirit may manifest in visions, whispers, or subtle movements within the reflection.

Step 3: Crafting the Spirit Amulet

Once the spirit has manifested and communion is complete, take the personal item and prepare to craft it into a permanent amulet. Speak directly to the spirit, offering it a place within the Reliquary Pendant or chosen amulet. Recite:

"By blood and bond, by love and will,
Thy spirit guard me still.
In this charm, I bind thee near,
To guide, to shield, to guard me here."

Carefully place the personal item into the Reliquary Pendant or amulet. A lock of hair, a small fragment of the beloved's keepsake, or another significant attachment can be placed within, creating a permanent bond between the spirit and the witch.

If you do not have a Reliquary Pendant, any sacred object that can house the personal item will serve as an excellent catalyst. The amulet will become a vessel for the spirit's presence, ensuring that the witch is guarded by the spirit in times of need.

Step 4: Sealing the Spell and the Amulet

To seal the spirit's presence within the amulet, anoint the amulet with Dark Moon Water, then pass it through the flame of the black candle. Speak the final words of the spell:

"In flame and water, earth and sky,
I bind thy spirit, never to fly.
Guard me now in all I do,
Until the time I summon you."

Let the amulet rest in the Magic Mirror's reflection for a few moments, allowing the spirit's essence to fully settle into its new home.

The Spirit Amulet, crafted through the Rite of the Spirit Speaker, is more than a simple charm – it is a guardian talisman imbued with the spirit of your deceased loved one. Whether housed in a

Reliquary Pendant or another personal object, the amulet acts as a vessel for the spirit's presence, offering protection, guidance, and companionship.

This powerful tool can be worn or carried, providing constant protection and guidance in all your workings. Through this rite, the witch ensures that the spirit will always walk beside them, shielding and guarding in times of need.

Spell for Safety while Traveling

This simple, practical spell is designed to protect the witch during their travels, ensuring safe passage and warding off any harm or misfortune. It draws upon the protective energy of the elements and invokes a protective charm that can be carried with you as a safeguard on your journey.

You Will Need:

- A small pouch (black or white for protection)
- A pinch of salt (for grounding and protection)
- A small protective stone (like black tourmaline, obsidian, or hematite)
- A dried bay leaf (for safety and victory)
- A small piece of sage or rosemary (for purification and protection)
- Optional: A personal token (such as a small charm or talisman for added connection)

Step 1: Preparing the Charm

1. Consecrate the Ingredients: Sit in a quiet space and lay out your ingredients. Hold the protective stone in your hand, visualizing it absorbing the power of the elements for your safety. Sprinkle the salt over the stone and say:

   "By salt and stone, protection strong,
   I call safe passage all day long.
   By earth's embrace and ground below,
   I travel safe where I shall go."

2. Add the Protective Herbs: Place the bay leaf and sage (or rosemary) in the pouch. These herbs carry the ancient power of protection, ensuring that you are shielded from harm. As you add them, say:

   "By leaf of bay and herb so pure,
   I call for safety to endure.
   No ill shall cross my path this day,
   By herb and will, I pave the way."

3. Place Your Personal Token (Optional): If you wish, place a small personal token (such as a charm or talisman) into the pouch, linking the spell's energy more directly to you.

Step 2: Sealing the Spell

1. Tie the Pouch: Once all ingredients are inside, tie the pouch securely. As you do, say the following words of protection:

   "By knot I seal this charm so tight,
   No harm shall touch, no fear alight.
   By road and path, by wheel and gate,
   I travel safe, by witch's fate."

Step 3: Carrying the Charm

- Carry the Charm with you whenever you are traveling – whether by car, plane, or foot. You can keep it in your pocket, bag, or vehicle as a constant source of protection.

Optional Additions:

- Bless the Pouch with a few drops of Full Moon Water for extra protective energy, calling upon the moon's light to guide your way.
- Anoint the Pouch with a drop of essential oil like lavender or frankincense to further imbue it with calming, protective energy.

Final Words:

Before you embark on your journey, take a moment to hold the charm in your hands and say:

"By charm and spell, I travel free,
No harm shall come, no ill to me.
By witch's will and spirit's guide,
I travel safe, by magic tied."

Tarot Divination

On the Green Path, divination is not simply about finding answers – it is a way to commune with the energies that flow through the natural and unseen worlds. Among the many tools in a witch's practice, tarot cards offer a profound way to reveal the light and shadow aspects of a situation. Just as the Twin Moons – the Full Moon and the Dark Moon – govern the cycles of revelation and concealment, tarot allows the witch to explore both the known and the hidden.

That said, tarot cards are not the only way to divine through cards. In cartomancy, a simple deck of playing cards can be used just as effectively as a tarot deck. Whether working with tarot or a standard deck of cards, the key is the witch's intention and the connection to the energies being consulted. As you work through this chapter, trust your intuition, and remember that it is the act of divination itself – not the specific tool – that brings insight.

In this chapter, three tarot spreads are provided to work with the powers of the Twin Moons, helping you navigate both light and shadow. Each spread offers a different approach, whether you seek clarity, need to uncover a hidden truth, or find balance between opposing forces. As you shuffle the cards, let the Full Moon and the Dark Moon guide your hand, illuminating the wisdom within.

Tarot Divination Spell: The Wisdom of the Twin Moons

This spell invites the guidance of the Full Moon and Dark Moon, using tarot (or a regular deck of cards) to reveal both the light and shadow aspects of a situation. The cards act as a conduit for the witch to see what is clear and what is concealed, drawing from the dual powers of the Twin Moons.

You Will Need:

- Your Tarot deck (or a deck of playing cards)
- A white candle (for the Full Moon's light)
- A black candle (for the Dark Moon's shadow)
- A bowl of Full Moon Water and a bowl of Dark Moon Water

Step 1: Preparing the Ritual Space

1. Light the White Candle: Place the white candle in the east, calling upon the Full Moon to bring light and clarity. This flame represents illumination, guiding the cards to reveal what is already known.
2. Light the Black Candle: Place the black candle in the west, where the Dark Moon reigns. This candle brings the shadows to light, helping to reveal what is hidden or unknown.
3. Bless the Water: Place the bowls of Full Moon Water and Dark Moon Water near their corresponding candles, representing the union of light and shadow in this divination.

Once the space is prepared, hold the deck of tarot or playing cards in your hands, allowing your mind to settle. Recite this incantation to invoke the wisdom of the Twin Moons:

> *"By moon of light and moon of dark,*
> *Reveal the truth, ignite the spark.*
> *By card and flame, both shadow and sight,*
> *I call on the wisdom of the night."*

The Tarot Spreads: Illuminating Light and Shadow

These spreads call on the Full Moon and Dark Moon to offer guidance. Whether seeking clarity, uncovering hidden truths, or balancing forces, these layouts will help the witch find the answers they seek.

Spread 1: The Veil of Shadows

When a truth remains hidden or a mystery needs uncovering, this spread draws on the Dark Moon's shadow to reveal what lies beneath the surface. This is particularly useful for when the witch feels a secret or concealed force is influencing the situation.

Layout:

1. What is hidden? – Card 1
2. What must be let go? – Card 2
3. What will be revealed? – Card 3

How to Perform:
Shuffle the cards while focusing on what feels obscured or uncertain. Lay out three cards in a triangle formation. The first card represents what is currently hidden, the second shows what you must release, and the third reveals what will come to light. Trust the Dark Moon to lift the veil in due time.

Spread 2: The Light of the Moon

When clarity is needed, this spread draws on the power of the Full Moon, illuminating the situation with its bright light. This spread is perfect for decision-making or when facing a crossroads.

Layout:

1. The situation at hand – Card 1
2. What influences this situation? – Card 2

3. What action must be taken? – Card 3
4. The outcome – Card 4

How to Perform:

As you shuffle the deck, focus on the question or decision you are facing. Lay out four cards in a straight line, letting the light of the Full Moon reveal the necessary steps. The cards represent the present situation, unseen influences, the action to take, and the outcome.

Spread 3: The Dance of the Twin Moons

This spread balances the light and shadow of any given situation, drawing on the powers of both the Full Moon and Dark Moon to show how the known and the unknown intertwine. It's particularly useful for exploring internal conflicts or navigating opposing forces.

Layout:

1. The Light (what is known) – Card 1
2. The Shadow (what is hidden) – Card 2
3. The Balance (how to unite them) – Card 3

How to Perform:

Shuffle the cards while focusing on a situation where balance is needed. Lay out three cards in a row. The first card shows what is already known, the second card reveals what is hidden, and the third card provides insight on how to bring these forces into balance. Trust in the Twin Moons to offer guidance on harmonizing light and shadow.

Closing the Spell

After your reading, take a moment to reflect on the messages received from the cards. Snuff out the candles and dip your fingers into the bowls of Full Moon Water and Dark Moon Water, sealing the balance of light and shadow into your divination.

Closing Incantation:

"I thank the moons, both light and dark,
For wisdom gained and visions stark.
By water sealed, by candle's flame,
I close the circle in their name."

Bone Casting: Osteomancy

In Green Witchcraft, the practice of Bone Casting (or Osteomancy) is a way to seek insight and guidance by connecting with the natural world. The bones used in this spell are not harvested, but rather ethically and naturally sourced – collected while exploring the wilds, often discovered as nature's offerings. These bones hold the energy of the earth, the creatures that once moved with them, and the deep, ancient knowledge of the cycles of life and death. It is this connection to the natural world that transmits the magic in Green Witchcraft.

You Will Need:

- A collection of naturally sourced bones (found while exploring nature, such as bird bones, small animal bones, or fish bones)
- A green cloth or earthy surface to cast the bones onto
- A quiet, outdoor space (or a place where you feel connected to nature)
- Optional: Herbs or flowers to bless the bones

    - Sage for wisdom and clarity
    - Lavender for calm and intuition
    - Rosemary for protection and focus

Step 1: Preparing the Bones

1. Cleansing and Honoring the Bones: Once you have naturally found your bones, spend time cleansing them

in a way that feels right to you. You can gently rinse them with water, smoke cleanse them with sage or herbs, or sprinkle them with Full Moon Water. As you cleanse the bones, honor the life they once carried and the spirit of the creature that has now passed.

"By earth and air, by root and bone,
I honor the life that you have known.
By moon and star, by fire and sea,
Your wisdom now speaks through me."

2. Charging the Bones with Intention: After cleansing the bones, hold them in your hands and focus on charging them with your intention. These bones are now sacred tools, connected to the cycles of nature, death, and rebirth. Visualize them being filled with the energy of the earth and the wisdom of the creatures that once moved with them.

Step 2: Setting the Sacred Casting Space

1. Prepare the Casting Surface: Lay down a green cloth or choose a natural surface (such as soil, stone, or a wooden table) that feels connected to the earth. This will be your sacred space for casting the bones. If you wish, sprinkle the area with herbs or lay down flowers to create a space of peace, intuition, and insight.
2. Create a Circle of Focus: Use your Witch's Broom or simply your hands to gently sweep the area, creating a circle that focuses the energy. This step helps you cast a sacred space, ensuring that the reading will be clear and guided by nature's wisdom.

"By broom and bone, I cast this ring,
The earth speaks now, to all I bring.
By wind and tree, by soil and sky,
The truth will rise, no more to hide."

Step 3: Casting the Bones

1. Formulate Your Question or Intention: Before casting the bones, focus on the question or area of life you seek insight into. The question should be clear in your mind, but feel free to ask open-ended questions as well (e.g., "What do I need to know about this situation?" or "What path should I follow?").
2. Cast the Bones: Holding the bones in your hands, stand over the prepared casting area. When you are ready, gently toss or scatter the bones onto the surface. Allow them to fall naturally, trusting that their placement holds the key to your answer. As you cast, say:

"By bone and breath, by root and sky,
Let nature speak, let truth not hide.
The bones will fall, the path be shown,
By earth's deep wisdom, I am known."

Step 4: Interpreting the Bones

1. Observe the Patterns: Once the bones have fallen, take a moment to observe how they've landed. The position, orientation, and proximity of the bones to each other will form the message. Look for patterns, groupings, or alignments, paying attention to what draws your eye first.

2. Interpret the Bones: The meaning of each bone will often depend on its size, shape, or the energy it carries from the animal it once belonged to. Here are some general guidelines for interpreting the bones:

    - Bones that fall near each other: This could indicate connected events or aspects of the question.
    - Bones that fall far apart: A sign of separation or distance in the situation.
    - Bones that point in a direction: A suggested path or course of action.
    - Bones that cross each other: A symbol of challenges, decisions, or blockages.

3. Use Your Intuition: Allow your intuition to guide you in reading the bones. Trust your inner sense of what each bone represents, as the energy of the bones and your connection to nature will transmit the message. Take time to reflect on the patterns, letting their meaning unfold.

Step 5: Closing the Reading

1. Thank the Bones and the Spirits of Nature: Once you've received the message, take a moment to thank the bones and the spirits of nature for their wisdom. This shows respect for the life that the bones once carried and for the earth's guidance in your divination.

    "By bone and earth, I give my thanks,
    To spirits wild, to nature's ranks.
    By life and death, by sun and sea,
    The truth revealed, so mote it be."

2. Store the Bones with Care: When you're done, carefully gather the bones and store them in a sacred pouch or a special box. Treat them with respect, knowing they are now infused with your energy and the wisdom of nature. These bones can be used again in future readings or rituals.

Crafting a Hex Bag

In the craft of the Green Witch, the Hex Bag serves as both a vessel of protection and concealment. Empowered by the shadows of the Dark Moon, this bag hides away the witch's most sacred tools from prying eyes, ensuring they remain unseen and untouched by unwanted forces. The Hex Bag is an ideal place to store tarot cards, casting bones, runes, or enchanted mirrors, protecting these divination tools from others who might gaze upon them and try to influence their magic. What is stored within the Hex Bag remains hidden, safely cloaked by the moonless night and further ensorcelled by a drop of the witch's own blood.

You Will Need:

- A small black or red bag (black for concealment, red for added protection)
- A bowl of Dark Moon Water
- A few sprigs of rosemary (for protection)
- A drop of your own blood (to seal the enchantment)
- Optional: anointing oil if aligned with your specific intent

Step 1: Preparing the Ritual Space

As this is a rite of concealment, perform the ritual in soft candlelight or darkness, honoring the quiet, hidden power of the Dark Moon. The Hex Bag will act as a shadowed vault, where none may gaze upon your sacred tools.

Step 2: Cleansing and Anointing the Bag

Hold the bag in your hands and gently anoint it with Dark Moon Water, invoking the shadow's power to guard and conceal.

As you do, speak this incantation to infuse it with the moon's protective energy:

"In shadow's fold, I hide this way,
Beneath the moon, where shadows sway.
By Dark Moon's grace, unseen, unknown,
I claim this bag as my hidden throne."

Place the rosemary inside the bag to fortify its protection and begin the next step.

Step 3: Ensorcelling the Hex Bag with Blood

To seal the Hex Bag with your own power, press a drop of your blood onto the fabric of the bag. This personal connection will bind the Hex Bag to you, ensuring that only your magic may unlock its secrets. Recite the following incantation as you offer the blood:

"With blood and shadow, I now bind,
This bag to hide what none may find.
By my will, unseen it be,
Locked from all but only me."

Visualize the blood's energy sealing the Hex Bag with its powerful, protective veil, guarding the items within from unwanted eyes.

Step 4: Charging the Hex Bag with the Dark Moon's Power

Now, take the bag and pass it above a candle flame, drawing on the energy of the Dark Moon to further conceal it in shadow. Be mindful not to touch the flame but allow the heat of the fire to activate the power of concealment. As you pass it through, recite:

"By flame unseen, I shield this place,
By moonless sky, I cloak this space.
No prying eye, no thief of sight,
May ever gaze upon this night."

Step 5: Using the Hex Bag

Once the ritual is complete, the Hex Bag is ready to receive the tools of your craft. Store tarot cards, casting bones, runes, or even enchanted mirrors within its depths, knowing they will remain hidden and guarded by the Dark Moon's shadow. The bag may also hold other sacred items, such as herbs, crystals, or charms that you wish to protect.

The Hex Bag can be recharged during each Dark Moon cycle by repeating this ritual, renewing its powers of protection and concealment.

The Witch's Dagger: Enchanting the Athame

The athame, or Witch's Dagger, is a sacred tool of gathering, protection, and direction. Unlike a mundane blade, it is not meant for physical cutting but for channeling energy and intention. The athame is the witch's sharpest tool, wielded in rituals to harness natural forces, protect against Malefica, and cut through the veil between worlds. The enchantment of the athame is a powerful ritual performed in two phases during the same lunar cycle – beginning with the Full Moon and ending with the New Moon.

In the Full Moon ritual, the athame catches the silver light of the moon over a bowl of water, connecting it with the gathering energies of nature and aligning it with the witch's will. During the Dark Moon ritual, the dagger is shrived clean over a candle flame, purging it of darkness and sharpening its protective edge. Together, these twin rituals charge the athame with the dual purpose of gathering from nature and guarding the witch against ill-intentioned spirits.

You Will Need:

- The athame (dagger) you wish to enchant
- A bowl of spring water (for the Full Moon ritual, reflecting the moon's light)
- A white candle (for the Dark Moon ritual)
- A silver ribbon or thread (to symbolize the moon's power)
- A dark stone such as obsidian or black tourmaline (for grounding and protection during the New Moon)
- A quiet outdoor space for both rituals, where you can feel the presence of the moon

The Full Moon Ritual: Catching the Moon's Light

The purpose of the Full Moon phase of the ritual is to gather the light and power of the moon, aligning the athame with the forces of nature. The Full Moon is a time of fullness, where energies are heightened, and the veil between realms is thinner. The blade will be imbued with the lunar power of gathering, attraction, and nature's rhythm.

Instructions:

1. Prepare Your Space: Go outside beneath the Full Moon, where the moonlight is strong. Find a spot where the moonlight reflects clearly in a bowl of spring water. This water will act as both a mirror and a conduit, pulling the light of the moon down to earth.
2. Casting the Circle: Use your Witch's Broom to sweep a sacred circle around your ritual space, clearing away any unwanted energies and protecting the space. As you sweep, say:

   "By broom and light, I cast this space,
   Beneath the moon, of silver grace."

3. Enchanting the Athame: Place your athame carefully over the bowl of water, allowing the blade to hover just above the surface. As the moonlight reflects on the water, focus on the blade drawing in the lunar energy. Hold the silver ribbon or thread, and as you weave it around the hilt of the athame, say:

   "By light of the moon, by water's grace,
   This blade I bless, to gather and trace.
   The forces of nature, wild and free,
   In this blade shall live, by moon's decree."

As you wrap the ribbon around the hilt, visualize the athame absorbing the moon's silver light, empowering it to draw strength from nature whenever you wield it. The water acts as a mirror, reflecting the power of the moon into the blade.

4. Sealing the Enchantment:
   Once the ribbon is secured, dip the tip of the blade lightly into the water, sealing the moon's energy into the athame. Whisper softly:

   "With silver light and water clear,
   I charge this blade, nature's power here."

5. Closing the Circle: Thank the moon for its guidance and protection, then carefully gather the water and pour it onto the earth as an offering. Sweep the circle counterclockwise to close it, saying:

   "By broom and moon, I release this space,
   The light remains, though time shall race."

The Dark Moon Ritual: Cleansing in Darkness

The Dark Moon marks the second phase of the enchantment, a time of cleansing and renewal. During this ritual, the athame is purified in the dark of the moon, its protective energies sharpened over the flame of a candle. The blade is shrived clean of any lingering shadows or energies, fortified to protect the witch from ill-intentioned spirits and dark forces.

Instructions:

1. Prepare Your Space: Find an outdoor space under the dark sky of the Dark Moon. Set your white candle before you,

and place the dark stone (obsidian or black tourmaline) next to it. The stone will ground the energies of protection as the dagger is enchanted.

2. Casting the Circle: Use your Witch's Broom once again to sweep a circle, creating a space of protection around you. As you sweep in the darkness, speak the following words:

   "By broom and dark, I cast this space,
   Beneath the night, a sacred place."

3. Cleansing the Athame: Light the white candle, the only light in the dark of the moon. Hold the athame above the flame, allowing the fire's heat to cleanse it. As the light flickers against the blade, say:

   "By flame of night, I burn away,
   All darkness cast, all shadows stray.
   This blade I cleanse, by fire's might,
   To guard my path, by sacred light."

   Visualize the blade being purified, its edge honed to protect against Malefica and malevolent spirits. Feel the flame's power sealing the blade's protective energies.

4. Sharpening the Athame's Purpose: Hold the athame close to your heart, feeling the dual energy of both the Full and Dark Moon – the gathering power from nature and the protective force from the dark. As you breathe, imagine these energies balancing within the blade, creating a perfect tool for your magical work.
5. Sealing the Enchantment: Let the candle burn a moment longer as you pass the blade over the flame one last time, whispering:

"With flame and night, this blade I seal,
A guard, a guide, and power real."

6. Closing the Ritual: Extinguish the candle, thanking the energies of the moon and flame. Release the circle with your broom, saying:

"By broom and dark, I release this space,
The power endures, in endless grace."

Place the athame safely in its sheath or on your altar, knowing that its twin enchantments are complete.

The Twin Enchantments: Full and New Moon in Harmony

These twin rituals, one performed under the Full Moon and the other under the Dark Moon, together complete the enchantment of the Witch's Dagger. The Full Moon ritual charges the athame with the power to gather from nature, to pull in energies and align them with the witch's purpose. The Dark Moon ritual cleanses and protects the athame, sharpening its power to defend against Malefica and banish harmful spirits.

In the balance between these two phases of the moon, the athame becomes both a tool of gathering and a shield of protection – perfectly attuned to the cycles of nature and the witch's will. Each time the blade is wielded, it carries the light of the moon and the fire of the night within it, a beacon and a shield, ever-present and always powerful.

The Witch's Cloak: Twin Moon Enchantment

This ritual calls upon the power of the Dark Moon – the time of concealment, protection, and hidden forces – to enchant the Witch's Cloak. By imbuing the cloak with the dark energy of the moon, the witch creates a powerful garment that shields them from prying eyes, both physical and spiritual, and empowers their magical workings. The cloak is named and baptized in Dark Moon Water, forever linking it to the unseen magic of the Dark Moon.

You Will Need:

- Your Witch's Cloak (preferably black or another dark color)
- A bowl of Dark Moon Water (prepared by collecting water under the New Moon)
- A black candle (to represent the Dark Moon)
- A small amount of salt (for grounding and purification)
- A quiet, dark space, preferably outdoors, or a room where you can see the sky
- Optional: Herbs such as mugwort, sage, or lavender for cleansing

Step 1: Preparing the Ritual Space

1. Cast the Circle with the Witch's Broom: Begin by sweeping the area with your Witch's Broom, symbolically clearing away any stagnant or negative energy. Focus on creating a sacred space where the power of the New Moon can be drawn down into your cloak. As you sweep, say:

"By broom and sweep, this space is clear,
No ill shall cross, no harm come near.
By circle cast in dark of night,
The moon's power hides me from sight."

2. Set the Elements: Place the black candle in the southern point of your circle (for fire), a small bowl of Dark Moon Water in the west (for water), a sprinkle of salt in the north (for earth), and leave space for the air at the east. This creates balance in your circle as you prepare to enchant your cloak.

Step 2: Naming the Cloak

1. Sit with the Cloak: Hold the cloak in your hands, close your eyes, and connect with its energy. Imagine the cloak as a protective barrier, one that shields you not only from physical elements but from unwanted energies and negative forces. Feel its weight and its fabric as an extension of your own magic.
2. Choose the Cloak's Name: Reflect on the cloak's purpose. What qualities do you want it to embody? What name calls to you that reflects its role in your magical practice? Allow a name to come to you, one that speaks to its power and identity. Once the name is clear, speak it aloud three times:

"By name I call you forth tonight,
Your form is veiled, concealed from sight.
[Cloak's Name], I give you breath and soul,
Your power now shall make me whole."

Step 3: Baptizing the Cloak in New Moon Water

1. Light the Black Candle: Light the black candle and place it near the bowl of Dark Moon Water. The flame represents the transformative energy of the dark moon, illuminating what is hidden, even in the darkest of nights.
2. Baptize the Cloak in Dark Moon Water: Gently dip the cloak into the Dark Moon Water, ensuring that it is baptized by the moon's dark energy. You may not fully submerge the cloak, but sprinkle the water over it, making sure the fabric absorbs the Dark Moon's power. As you do this, say:

   "By moon unseen, by water's dark,
   I bless this cloak, I leave my mark.
   By moonless sky and shadow deep,
   This cloak shall guard when others sleep."

Visualize the cloak absorbing the energy of the Dark Moon, becoming a veil of protection and concealment that you can wear in your magical workings.

Step 4: Sealing the Enchantment

1. Anoint the Cloak with Salt: After baptizing the cloak, take a pinch of salt and sprinkle it lightly over the fabric. The salt grounds the cloak's magic in the earth, giving it stability and protection. As you sprinkle the salt, say:

   "By earth and salt, your power grows,
   No harm shall find me where I go.

Your weave is strong, your purpose clear,
I walk in shadow, none come near."

2. Hold the Cloak to the Black Candle: Pass the cloak near the black candle flame, allowing the fire to seal the enchantment. Be careful not to burn the cloak – this step symbolizes imbuing the cloak with the element of fire for strength and power. As you do this, say:

   "By fire's light and moon's dark veil,
   This cloak shall hide me without fail.
   By flame and night, by smoke and sea,
   This cloak is sealed, so mote it be."

Step 5: Wearing the Enchanted Cloak

1. Drape the Cloak Over Your Shoulders: Now that the cloak is named, baptized, and sealed with moon and fire, drape it over your shoulders. Feel its weight and energy wrapping around you, offering both protection and concealment. When you wear this cloak, know that you are hidden from harmful forces and empowered in your magic.
2. Recite the Final Incantation: Stand in your circle, wearing the cloak, and recite the final incantation to solidify the connection between you and the cloak:

   "By cloak of dark and moonless sky,
   I walk unseen, no harm draws nigh.
   By Dark Moon's power, I am concealed,
   My will is strong, my fate is sealed."

Step 6: Closing the Ritual

1. Thank the Elements: Offer thanks to the elements for their assistance in the enchantment. Acknowledge the New Moon's energy for its protection and wisdom. Blow out the black candle and say:

   "My thanks I give, to moon and night,
   To flame and salt, and circle bright.
   The spell is done, the charm is made,
   In shadows deep, I stand unafraid."

2. Store the Cloak: When not in use, store the cloak in a sacred place, perhaps with other magical tools. Keep it in the dark to retain its connection to the Dark Moon's power. Use the cloak during rituals, spells, or anytime you need protection or wish to remain unseen.

Crafting the Witch's Girdle

This sacred spell draws upon the power of the Twin Moons – the Full Moon's radiant shield and the Dark Moon's shadowed cloak – crafting a Witch's Girdle that binds protection from both light and dark forces. Through this rite, the girdle becomes a potent ward, safeguarding the witch from malefic harm, while balancing the powers of revelation and concealment. The magic is set through dual enchantments beneath the Full and Dark Moons, and solidified in the cauldron, ensuring the girdle shields the witch from all forces – be they seen or unseen.

Full Moon Incantation:

"Circle of the Whitest Moon,
Imbue in thee, a holy boon,
Protection around, a spirit within,
Shield me on journeys, guard me from sin.
By light of day and darkest night,
Guard my path, keep me from sight."

Dark Moon Incantation:

"Circle of the Darkest Night,
Cloak my steps, conceal my light.
From shadow deep, no harm shall pass,
Guard me with thy moonlit cast.
Shielded here, hidden from sight,
By moonless sky, in shadowed flight."

Step 1: The Rite of the Full Moon

Begin beneath the Full Moon's light, with the Witch's Girdle – a length of cord or woven fabric – laid upon the altar or under the moon's direct gaze. Recite the Full Moon Incantation, calling upon the bright and protective radiance of the Whitest Moon. With each word spoken, envision the girdle absorbing the moon's light, becoming a shield to guard your path from harm.

Once the spell is spoken, anoint the girdle with Dark Moon Water, balancing the clarity of the Full Moon with the concealed power of the Dark Moon. Let the girdle rest in the Full Moon's glow throughout the night, soaking in the protective energy of the Twin Moons.

Step 2: The Rite of the Dark Moon

On the night of the Dark Moon, return to your sacred space. Under the veil of night's shadow, recite the Dark Moon Incantation, this time calling upon the hidden power of the Dark Moon to cloak and conceal your presence from malefic forces. As you speak the spell, envision the girdle wrapping you in an invisible shield, protecting you from all who would seek to harm or spy upon you.

Once the incantation is complete, anoint the girdle with Full Moon Water, ensuring that the energies of both light and shadow are entwined. The girdle now holds the balanced powers of both the Whitest Moon and the Darkest Night, a duality of protection that shields you in all realms.

Step 3: Resting the Girdle in the Cauldron

After the girdle has been imbued with the powers of the Twin Moons, it must rest to allow the magic to take full hold. Coil the Witch's Girdle and place it in the cauldron for three days. The cauldron, symbolizing transformation and protection, will hold the girdle as it solidifies the spells cast upon it. To deepen the magic, you may choose to tie knots into the girdle, each knot imbued with your protective intentions – whether for warding off danger, securing secrecy, or guarding your journeys.

Add sacred herbs – such as rosemary for protection, mugwort for vision, or sage for purification – into the cauldron to further bless the girdle. These herbs will lend their powers to the spell, enhancing the girdle's magic

Ritual of Familiar Enchantment

This ritual consecrates your pet as your familiar, deepening the bond between you and your animal companion, offering protection, and acknowledging its role as your guide to the natural world. In this rite, your familiar becomes more than a companion – it becomes a magical partner, attuned to the energies you work with and serving as a spiritual protector.

You Will Need:

- Your Witch's Broom (previously enchanted for cleansing and protection)
- A white candle (for purity and connection)
- A green candle (for protection, life, and nature)
- A small bowl of spring water (to symbolize the flow of energy between you and your familiar)
- Dried lavender or rosemary (for protection and calming energies)
- A piece of hematite or black tourmaline (for grounding and protection of the familiar)
- A token that symbolizes your bond with your pet (such as a collar, toy, or piece of fabric)
- A few drops of essential oil (such as lavender or chamomile, which is safe for animals)

Preparation:

1. Cleanse your space using your Witch's Broom. Sweep in a clockwise motion, visualizing the removal of any stagnant or negative energy from the area. As you sweep, say:

"By broom and herb, I sweep away,
All that hinders cannot stay.
I cleanse all Evil from this space,
from this time, and from this space.
No Evil thing may harm me here,
be it far or be it near."

2. As you cleanse, feel the space around you becoming lighter, more open to magic, and ready to hold the energy of your bond with your familiar.
3. Set the candles on either side of you:

    - Place the white candle to represent purity and the clarity of your bond.
    - Place the green candle to represent nature and protection.

4. Light the candles and place the bowl of spring water in front of you and your pet. Scatter the dried lavender or rosemary around the bowl and candles to bring calming energy to the space.

Step 1: Casting the Circle with the Witch's Broom

With your enchanted broom in hand, walk the perimeter of the space in a clockwise direction, sweeping lightly to cast the circle. As you walk, visualize the creation of a protective, sacred circle around you and your pet, a barrier of light that strengthens your bond and wards off any harmful energies. While sweeping, chant:

"By broom and might, I cast this space,
A circle strong, of love and grace.

No harm shall pass, no ill shall near,
Within this circle, all is clear."

Once the circle is cast, place your broom at the side of the ritual space, brush-end facing west (for water, emotion, and intuition) and staff-end pointing east (for air, wisdom, and new beginnings).

Step 2: Consecrating Your Pet as a Familiar

Sit beside your pet, placing your hands gently on them. Close your eyes and breathe deeply, focusing on the connection between the two of you. Feel the energy flowing from you to your pet and from your pet to you, creating a loop of shared understanding and trust. As you connect, speak the following words:

"By fur, by feather, by scale, or skin,
I call thee now to bond within.
Familiar true, my guide, my friend,
I name you now! Loyalty-That-Knows-No-End!
In this Sacred Holy Hour with you, I find my witch's power!
Protector strong in every space,
With love and trust, bound spirits embrace,
Familiar (insert pet name), you are mine
And I am yours for all of time!
To serve, to guide, to herd, to flock,
May now never be apart!
In the name of the Moon,
In the name of the Sea,
In the name of our bond,
So mote it be! "

As you say these words, visualize a golden thread of energy wrapping around both you and your familiar, sealing your bond and opening the channels of communication and understanding between you.

Step 3: Anointing and Blessing

Take the bowl of spring water and add a few drops of essential oil. Stir it clockwise three times, saying:

"Water of life, flow between us,
Anoint this bond with sacred trust."

Dip your fingers in the water and gently anoint your pet by placing a small amount of water on their head, paws, or chest – whichever area feels comfortable and natural for your companion. As you anoint them, say:

"By water's grace, I bless thee now,
To walk beside me, show me how.
In forest, field, and skies above,
You are my guide, my strength, my love."

Afterward, gently anoint your own forehead and hands with the same water, symbolizing the shared journey between you and your familiar.

Step 4: Offering Protection

Place the hematite or black tourmaline near your pet, or tie it loosely to their collar or keep it in their sleeping space, imbuing it with the power of protection. Hold the stone in your hand and speak:

"With this stone, I call to ground,
Protect my familiar, safe and sound.
No harm shall come, no ill shall pass,
For we are one, a bonded mass."

Visualize a protective barrier forming around your pet, strong and steady, guarding them against negative forces while keeping their spirit light and free. Feel the energy of the earth anchoring them in safety.

Step 5: Closing the Ritual

Take the token of your bond – a collar, a toy, or another personal item – and hold it between your hands. Infuse it with your intention, focusing on the deepened connection between you and your familiar. You can offer it to your pet, or simply keep it as a reminder of this ritual. As you hold the token, say:

"In this token, I place my trust,
Our bond eternal, strong and just.
By moon and sun, by earth and sky,
Familiar true, by my side, you fly."

When you feel the ritual is complete, thank the elements for their presence:

"By Air, I release this space,
By Fire, I ignite our grace,
By Water, I flow with love,
By Earth, protection from above.
Our circle is open, yet unbroken.
As I will, so mote it be."

Take your broom and sweep the circle counterclockwise to close the space, lifting the circle and returning the energies to their natural state. As you sweep, say:

"With broom in hand, I now release,
The circle fades, but not our peace.

Our bond endures, our path is sure,
Protected, strong, and ever pure."

Extinguish the candles, and allow the energies of the ritual to settle around both you and your familiar.

Deepening the Bond

This ritual not only consecrates your pet as a familiar but also deepens the natural bond between you, aligning your magical paths and placing protections upon your animal companion. The familiar now stands as a guide to the natural world, attuned to the cycles of the earth and the magic that flows through it. As your familiar walks beside you, they bring wisdom, protection, and a deeper connection to the wild energies you work with.

Charm for Soothing Animals

Purpose:

This charm is used to soothe and calm animals, particularly when preparing to assist them or when deepening the bond with a familiar.

Instructions:

1. Approach the animal gently and begin caressing them with slow, calming movements.
2. While doing so, softly repeat the following incantation:

   "Ah jhee vah mee she mah"
   (Note: This is a phonetic translation of the original phrase, traditionally pronounced slowly and with intention. Allow the soothing rhythm to resonate as you speak.)

3. If you are working with a familiar, you may enhance the connection by pressing your forehead to theirs as you continue to repeat the incantation.
4. Focus on the bond between you and the animal, letting the connection deepen as the soothing energy flows from you to them.

Notes:

- This charm is particularly useful in moments of stress or tension and can be repeated as needed until the animal appears calm and at ease.
- For familiars, the forehead-to-forehead contact can intensify the sense of connection, trust, and shared understanding.

The Ancient Art of Elemental Witchcraft

In the deep roots of Traditional Witchcraft, witches have always sought to form an intimate connection with the natural world. The forces of Earth, Air, Fire, and Water are not mere metaphors but living, breathing entities – each with its own temper, its own spirit, its own will. Through centuries of practice, witches have learned to invoke, honor, and command these elements, calling upon them to lend their power to spells, rituals, and magical workings.

This collection of Elemental Spells draws upon those ancient rites, the whispers of hedge witches, the secrets of forest-dwelling wise women, and the folk traditions passed down through the ages. Each spell carries with it the weight of tradition and the power of the elements, with the words carefully chosen to echo the voices of the Old Craft.

To work with the elements is to align oneself with nature's rhythm, to tap into the deep wells of energy that flow through all things. Whether you seek to ground yourself with Earth's enduring strength, to stir the winds of Air for clarity, to ignite the fires of courage, or to heal with Water's flowing grace, these spells call upon the very forces that shape our world.

Earth Element Spells

The Earth element is a symbol of steadfastness, manifestation, and protection. It is the fertile ground from which all things grow, and the stone foundation upon which the world rests. To invoke Earth is to call upon the power of roots – both literal and metaphorical – digging deep into the soil to draw sustenance, strength, and stability.

Spell for Prosperity and Abundance

In this spell, the witch calls upon the abundant spirit of Earth, whose fertile soil brings forth bounty and riches. With offerings of coin, soil, and herbs that carry the ancient energy of wealth, this spell plants the seeds of prosperity, trusting the earth to nurture and bring them to fruition.

You Will Need:

- A small green candle (blessed for wealth and growth)
- A silver coin (to represent the richness of the earth)
- A small bowl of soil (gathered from a place of power – your garden, a forest, or crossroads)
- Dried basil (to attract wealth and abundance)
- A pinch of cinnamon (to speed the manifestation)

How to Perform It:

1. Consecrate the Space: Begin by casting a circle. Sweep the space with your Witch's Broom, invoking the protective spirits of the Earth. Feel the grounding energy beneath you.

   "By broom and dust, by earth and clay,
   I call the Earth to work today.
   This space is cleansed, this spell begun,
   Prosperity flows where the spell is spun."

2. Light the Green Candle: Light the green candle, its flame a beacon of wealth and abundance. Place it next to the bowl of soil, feeling the energy of growth rising with the flame.
3. Offer the Coin to the Earth: Hold the coin in your hands and feel the energy of wealth flowing through you. Speak to the Earth, asking for its blessing, and say:

   "By silver's gleam and green flame bright,
   I call forth wealth into my sight.

By earth's deep heart and coin in hand,
Prosperity flows throughout the land."

4. Plant the Coin in the Soil: Gently place the coin in the bowl of soil, symbolizing the planting of your intention. Sprinkle the basil and cinnamon over the soil, invoking the ancient powers of growth and abundance.

   "With basil's green and cinnamon's spice,
   I call forth gold, my life entice.
   By earth's rich hand, by root and seed,
   The coin I plant fulfills my need."

5. Let the Candle Burn: Allow the candle to burn down safely, visualizing the seeds of prosperity taking root, growing strong and steady in the soil of your intention.
6. Leave the Coin in the Soil: Once the candle has burned down, leave the coin in the soil and place it on your altar or in a safe space. The coin, buried like a seed, will continue to grow and manifest your desires for prosperity.

Spell for Grounding and Stability

In this spell, the witch seeks the grounding power of the Earth, calling upon the steady energy of stone and soil to bring balance, calm, and security. This is an ancient rite to anchor oneself to the Earth, to find stillness in the swirling winds of life.

You Will Need:

- A small brown stone (such as hematite or jasper, for grounding)
- A bowl of salt (for purity and protection)
- A piece of wood or bark (symbolizing roots and stability)

How to Perform It:

1. Create a Sacred Space: Sit upon the earth, if possible, or find a quiet place where you feel connected to nature. Place the bowl of salt before you, and hold the stone in your hands.

   "By salt of earth and stone of might,
   I call the ground to hold me tight.
   By tree and root, by earth and bone,
   I ground my soul, I stand alone."

2. Call Upon the Roots: Visualize roots growing from your body, sinking deep into the earth. Feel the energy of the earth pulling you down, grounding you, making you strong and immovable. Hold the stone to your chest, letting its energy anchor you.
3. Speak the Incantation: As you hold the stone, say:

   "By earth and root, I stand secure,
   My mind is calm, my heart is sure.
   By stone's deep heart and wood's firm hand,
   The earth shall hold where I shall stand."

4. Place the Stone in Salt: Place the stone in the bowl of salt, sealing the grounding energy. The salt represents purity, the stone stability – together, they create a shield of protection and strength around you.
5. Carry the Stone: Carry the stone with you in times of uncertainty or when you feel ungrounded. It will serve as a reminder of your connection to the earth, always available to anchor you when life feels chaotic.

Air Element Spells

The Air element is the breath of life, the whisper of thought, the song of the wind through the trees. It is the element of clarity, communication, and freedom. Witches who work with Air invoke the winds of change, the power of the mind to bring forth clarity and insight. Air carries the magic of vision and understanding, of dreams and whispers in the night.

Spell for Clarity and Mental Focus

This spell uses the lightness of Air to clear away mental fog, promote focus, and open the mind to sharp and clear thinking. Through the power of the wind and the aid of herbs that sharpen the senses, this spell will lift confusion and allow insight to flow freely.

You Will Need:

- A small yellow candle (for clarity and illumination)
- A feather (to represent the movement of air)
- Dried mint (for mental sharpness)
- Dried lavender (to calm and clarify)

How to Perform It:

1. Cast a Circle of Air: Begin by casting a circle. Move clockwise, feeling the breeze stir the space around you. Light the yellow candle, its flame representing the clarity of thought and the light of insight.

   "By air's sweet breath and candle's light,
   I call the winds to bring me sight.
   By circle cast and mind made clear,
   Let truth be seen, let doubt draw near."

2. Invoke the Winds: Hold the feather in your hand, feeling its lightness. Visualize the winds sweeping through your mind, clearing away the fog. Sprinkle the dried mint and lavender around the candle, invoking the sharpness of thought and the calm clarity of vision.
3. Speak the Words of Clarity: As you hold the feather, say:

"By wind and sky, my mind is free,
No fog shall hold, no doubt shall be.
By mint's bright leaf and lavender's calm,
My mind is sharp, my thoughts are strong."

4. Let the Wind Take Your Doubt: Allow the candle to burn as you meditate on the flame. Visualize the winds carrying away your doubts, leaving only clarity in their wake. Breathe deeply, inhaling the fresh air, exhaling confusion and uncertainty.
5. Use the Feather as a Charm: Once the spell is complete, keep the feather on your altar or carry it with you as a charm for clarity and insight. It will serve as a reminder to remain open and clear-minded in all situations.

Fire Element Spells

The Fire element is the spark of creation and destruction, the energy of transformation and passion. Fire is both feared and revered for its ability to consume and purify. Witches working with Fire invoke its light, heat, and raw power to ignite change, banish negativity, and empower their intentions with strength and will. Fire is fast, fierce, and unyielding – once called upon, it demands the witch's full attention and respect.

Spell for Courage and Inner Strength

This spell draws on the fierce energy of Fire to ignite the flame of courage within the witch's heart. It is a spell of power, calling upon the wrathful yet protective force of Fire to burn away fear and hesitation, leaving only the strength to face challenges with confidence. The ancient rites of fire bring transformation, burning away doubt and replacing it with the unshakable force of will.

You Will Need:

- A red candle (for courage and strength)
- A cinnamon stick (to enhance the fiery energy)
- A small dish of ash (symbolizing transformation and the power of Fire)
- Optional: Dried ginger root or cloves (to intensify the spell's power)

How to Perform It:

1. Cast the Circle of Fire: Begin by casting your circle, but this time, circle the space three times with your Witch's Broom, sweeping the air to clear the energy. As you move, visualize a ring of flames rising around you, a protective circle of fire that will aid in your transformation.

   "By flame and ash, this circle cast,
   No fear may enter, none shall last.
   By broom and air, the fire's light,
   I call my strength within this night."

2. Light the Red Candle: Place the red candle in the center of your circle and light it, focusing on the fierce flame. As it flickers and grows, see the flame as the courage that will grow within you. The flame is your inner strength, untouchable by doubt or fear.

3. Chant the Incantation for Courage: Hold the cinnamon stick over the flame, feeling its warmth in your hands. As you do, say:

   "By fire's heat and flame so bright,
   I call my courage in this night.
   No fear may bind, no doubt shall stay,
   My heart burns fierce, as bright as day."

4. Anoint the Ashes: Take a small pinch of ash and sprinkle it around the base of the candle, saying:

   "By fire's ash, by flame's last breath,
   I rise from fear, I stand from death.
   No harm may come, no fear may last,
   I am the fire, my will holds fast."

5. Visualize Your Courage: Sit quietly and watch the flame of the candle as it burns, imagining your inner fire growing stronger with every flicker. Let the cinnamon intensify the heat, feeling its fiery energy pulse through your veins. Envision yourself standing tall, fearless and unshakable, as the flame of courage burns away all fear.
6. Extinguish the Candle: When you are ready, extinguish the candle, but do so with purpose. As you snuff the flame, say:

   "By fire's end, my strength remains,
   No fear may touch, no doubt may reign.
   My courage burns, my heart is strong,
   I stand in power, I shall belong."

7. Carry the Ash: Keep a small pinch of the ash in a pouch, or sprinkle it on yourself as a charm of inner strength. It

will serve as a reminder of your courage and the power of Fire that now burns within you.

Water Element Spells

The Water element is the source of life, healing, and intuition. It is the fluid and ever-changing force of emotion, dreams, and spiritual depth. Water flows through all things, carrying both healing energy and the power to cleanse what is impure or stagnant. Witches who work with Water tap into the mysteries of the unseen and the unknown, invoking the deep waters of the subconscious to bring healing, intuition, and transformation.

Spell for Emotional Healing

This spell uses the gentle but powerful energy of Water to heal emotional wounds and restore inner peace. Water is called upon to wash away pain, grief, or heartache, leaving the witch renewed and whole. Like the ancient healing springs, this spell invokes the element of Water as a source of spiritual and emotional cleansing.

You Will Need:

- A small bowl of moon water (collected under the Full Moon for extra potency)
- Dried rose petals (for emotional healing and love)
- Dried chamomile (for peace and soothing)
- A blue candle (representing Water and healing energy)

How to Perform It:

1. Prepare the Sacred Waters: Begin by lighting the blue candle and placing it beside the bowl of moon water. As you do, imagine the waters glowing with the light of the

Full Moon, blessed for healing. Hold the bowl in your hands, focusing on the energy of peace and renewal that it carries.

"By moon's soft glow and water's grace,
I call forth healing in this space.
By river's flow and ocean's might,
Let pain dissolve into the night."

2. Add the Healing Herbs: Sprinkle the rose petals and chamomile into the water, letting them float on the surface. As you do, speak their purpose aloud:

"By rose's bloom, my heart shall mend,
By chamomile's peace, my wounds shall end.
By water's grace and moonlight bright,
I heal my soul this sacred night."

3. Chant the Incantation for Healing: Dip your fingers into the water and gently sprinkle it over your heart, or wherever you feel emotional pain. As you do, say:

"By water's flow, let pain be gone,
By moon's soft light, my soul is drawn.
With every drop, I heal my heart,
By water's grace, new life shall start."

4. Visualize the Healing Waters: Sit quietly, holding the bowl of water, and visualize the healing energy flowing through your body, washing away all grief and emotional pain. See the water cleansing your spirit, leaving only peace and light behind. Let the rose and chamomile infuse your heart with their gentle energy.

5. Anoint Yourself with the Water: After the meditation, use the water to anoint your forehead, heart, and hands. Feel the healing power sealing within you, filling you with renewal and peace.
6. Keep the Water: Once the spell is complete, you can keep the remaining water in a vial or bottle as a charm of healing. Anoint yourself with it whenever you feel emotional wounds resurface, allowing the magic of Water to continue its work.

Spell for Purification and Spiritual Cleansing

In this spell, the witch calls upon the cleansing power of Water to purify their spirit and release any negative or stagnant energy. Water is invoked as a sacred purifier, washing away all that no longer serves, leaving the spirit cleansed and free.

You Will Need:

- A bowl of pure water (from a natural source if possible)
- Dried sage (for purification)
- A pinch of sea salt (for grounding and protection)
- A white candle (symbolizing spiritual purity)

How to Perform It:

1. Create a Circle of Water: Light the white candle and place it near the bowl of water. Begin by sprinkling a pinch of salt around the space, creating a circle of protection. As you do, invoke the protective spirits of Water:

   "By salt and sea, this circle's cast,
   No ill may stay, no harm shall last.
   By water's might and sage's flame,
   I call this space, pure in its name."

2. Purify the Water: Hold the bowl of water in your hands and sprinkle the dried sage into it. Speak to the Water, calling upon it to cleanse your spirit and wash away any negativity:

   "By water's flow, by sage's leaf,
   I call this spell to bring relief.
   By salt and sea, by wave and light,
   I cleanse my soul within this night."

3. Chant the Incantation for Purification: Dip your fingers into the water and anoint your forehead, heart, and hands, saying:

   "By water pure and sage's fire,
   I cleanse my soul of ill desire.
   No harm may stay, no shadow near,
   My spirit's clean, my mind is clear."

4. Visualize the Cleansing: Close your eyes and imagine the water flowing over you, washing away all negativity, stagnant energy, and impurities. Feel the water purifying your spirit, leaving you light, clear, and renewed.
5. Complete the Ritual: After the ritual, you can pour the remaining water outside, offering it back to the earth as a symbol of the cleansing that has taken place. Let the white candle burn down, signifying the purity restored.

Summoning a Storm

Traditional Folk Witch Practices and a Spell to Invoke the Wrathful Elements

In folk witchcraft traditions, summoning storms has long been associated with elemental magic, particularly invoking the wrathful aspects of nature. Storm witches, sea witches, and other practitioners of weather magic would call upon the elements to stir the winds, bring rain, or unleash a storm's fury. Traditionally, the ability to summon a storm was linked to the relationship between the witch and the natural elements – a deep connection to the land, sky, and sea. Below are some traditional ways folk witches would summon storms, followed by a spell designed to invoke the wrath of the elements and call forth a storm.

Traditional Ways Folk Witches Summon Storms

1. **Witch's Knots and Wind Binding**

- One of the most traditional methods for summoning winds and storms involved knot magic. Witches would tie knots in a cord while chanting to bind or release the wind. By tying three knots in a cord and calling upon the winds from the four cardinal directions, the witch could summon a storm.
- The knots could be untied one by one to release the winds, each knot representing a different level of intensity.

2. **Casting a Charm into Water**

- Some sea witches would cast a charm or stone into the ocean or a body of water while invoking the spirits of the sea and sky to raise a storm. The tossing of an object into the water was symbolic of stirring the sea, calling upon the elements of water and air to join forces and bring a storm.

- This could also be done with storm water (water collected during a storm), which could be poured into the earth or back into the sea to reawaken the storm's energy.

3. **Dancing in the Wind**

- Witches would sometimes dance in the wind, using their bodies to channel the energy of the elements. By spinning and moving with the air, the witch would "weave" the wind around them, encouraging it to gather strength and bring the storm's full force.

4. **Calling on Elemental Spirits**

- In many traditions, witches would call upon the elemental spirits of air, water, and fire to stir the atmosphere and summon a storm. These spirits were seen as living forces that could be entreated or commanded to bring about natural changes, especially powerful storms.
- Offerings would sometimes be made to these elemental forces – herbs, salt, or stones – to honor them and ensure they cooperated.

Rite of the Storm Caller

This calls the powers of the elements to invoke the wrathful aspects of their powers and domains – air, water, fire, and earth – to summon a storm. The witch calls upon the winds to rise, the waters to swell, and the lightning to strike, creating a fierce display of nature's power. This spell should be approached with caution and respect for the elements, as it calls forth natural forces that are not easily controlled.

You Will Need:

- A cord or red ribbon (for knot magic)
- A bowl of storm water (collected from a previous storm) or sea water (if available)
- A black candle (to represent the destructive power of fire and lightning)
- A small dish of salt (for grounding and connecting to the earth)
- Optional: Feathers (for air), stones (for earth), herbs like mugwort or sage (for offerings to the elements)

Step 1: Casting the Circle of the Elements

1. Begin by Casting the Circle: Using your Witch's Broom, sweep the area to clear it of any lingering energy. As you sweep, you are preparing to call upon the wrathful forces of the elements.

"By broom and sky, by earth and sea,
I clear this space, my will is free.
The winds shall rise, the storm endures,
By witch's hand, the elements I stir."

2. Place the Elements in the Circle: Place your bowl of storm water or sea water in the west (for water). Place a small dish of salt in the north (for earth). The black candle should be placed in the south (for fire). Leave the east for air and wind, perhaps symbolized by feathers or a light breeze.

Step 2: Invoking the Wrathful Elements

1. Tie the First Knot – Calling the Winds: Take your cord or red ribbon and tie the first knot while facing east. As you tie it, call upon the winds to rise and stir. Feel the air around you gathering energy, ready to rush forward.

   "By east wind's breath and rising gale,
   The storm shall rise, the winds shall wail.
   By knot of air, I bind and call,
   The winds obey, let tempests fall."

2. Tie the Second Knot – Stirring the Waters: Face west, holding the cord, and tie the second knot, this time invoking the waters to swell and surge. Feel the pull of the ocean or stormy rain gathering force.

   "By western sea and water's flow,
   I call the rains, let torrents grow.
   By knot of water, I stir the tide,
   The waves shall rise, and my will abide."

3. Tie the Third Knot – Awakening Fire: Face south, lighting the black candle to represent lightning and fire. Tie the third knot, summoning the lightning to strike and the storm to bring its fiery energy.

"By southern flame and lightning's crack,
The skies shall roar, the clouds go black.
By knot of fire, the storm shall burn,
The sky alight, no calm return."

4. Ground the Spell with Earth: Finally, face north and place your hands on the ground, feeling the solid energy of earth beneath you. Call upon the earth to ground and stabilize the storm's energy, ensuring that it is controlled and directed. Say:

   "By northern earth, by mountain's might,
   The storm shall churn, the storm shall bite.
   By earth I ground, by stone I call,
   The storm to rise, and elements to fall."

Step 3: Summoning the Storm

1. Pour the Storm Water: Pour a few drops of storm water or sea water into the earth at the center of your circle, calling forth the storm to awaken. As you pour the water, visualize the clouds gathering, the winds rising, and the rain beginning to fall.

   "By water's surge and sky's great tear,
   I call the storm, I rend the air.
   By lightning's strike and roaring sea,
   The storm shall rise, so mote it be."

2. Untie the Knots: One by one, untie the knots in your cord to release the storm. As you untie each knot, visualize the elements obeying your command – first the winds, then the waters, and finally the fire of lightning. With each release, say:

"I free the winds, let storm clouds rise.
I free the waters, let the rain baptize.
I free the fire, let the skies ignite.
By elements' wrath, let the storm take flight."

Step 4: Closing the Ritual

1. Thank the Elements: After the storm has been summoned, or after the ritual is complete, thank the elements for their power and presence. It is essential to acknowledge and honor their strength, as storm magic is unpredictable and requires deep respect.

   "To wind and wave, to fire and stone,
   My thanks I give for power shown.
   By storm's great might, I honor thee,
   I close this spell, so mote it be."

2. Extinguish the Candle and Ground the Energy: Extinguish the black candle, representing the fire and lightning returning to rest. Place your hands on the ground once more to ground the energy of the storm spell, ensuring that the spell's energy is contained and properly released.

Respecting the Elements in Storm Magic

Summoning a storm is one of the most powerful and dangerous forms of elemental magic. It taps into the uncontrollable forces of nature, so it must be performed with caution and respect. Folk witches who summoned storms often had strong relationships with the land and sea, and they understood the delicate balance between calling upon the elements and honoring their unpredictable nature.

The Witch's Bottle

This Witch's Bottle is a tried a true element of Traditional Witchcraft. The spell serves as a powerful ward against harmful intentions, negative energy, and unwanted spiritual forces. By crafting this bottle and filling it with protective elements from nature, the witch creates a shield of protection that guards both the physical and spiritual realms. Once sealed and hidden, the bottle will work quietly to absorb and neutralize any malefic energy directed toward you or your home.

You Will Need:

- A small glass bottle or jar with a sealable lid
- Rusty nails or iron tacks (to deflect negativity)
- Sea salt (for purification and protection)
- Black tourmaline or obsidian (for grounding and protection)
- Herbs for protection:
    - Rosemary (for warding off evil)
    - Sage (for purification)
    - Thyme (for strength and protection)
    - Bay leaves (for success and protection)
- A small personal item (like a hair strand or a nail clipping, to link the bottle to you)
- Full Moon Water or Dark Moon Water (depending on the nature of the protection you seek)
- Optional: Thorns, pins, or broken glass for additional warding strength
- A black candle for sealing the bottle

- Wax to seal the bottle shut (from the black candle or another candle of your choice)

Step 1: Preparing the Bottle

1. Cleanse the Bottle: Before you begin filling the bottle, cleanse it with Full Moon Water or sage smoke to ensure it's free of any previous energy. Hold the bottle in your hands, focusing on your intention of protection. You may say:

   "By moon's light and water clear,
   I cleanse this vessel, pure and dear.
   Let it hold no harm or ill,
   Its purpose pure, my will to still."

2. Gather Your Ingredients: Assemble all your ingredients and make sure you are in a quiet, sacred space where you can focus on your intention for the bottle. Lay everything out in front of you.

Step 2: Filling the Witch's Bottle

1. Add the Rusty Nails and Iron Tacks: Begin by placing a few rusty nails or iron tacks into the bottle. These items are traditional protective elements that serve to deflect harmful energy. As you drop them into the bottle, visualize them acting as a barrier to any negative forces.

   "By iron's edge and rusted thorn,
   I trap all ill and stop the scorn.
   No harm shall cross this blessed line,
   My home is safe, my will divine."

2. Add the Sea Salt: Next, pour in sea salt, which purifies and protects. Salt is known for its ability to absorb negative energy and create a protective boundary. As you add the salt, say:

   "By salt of sea, I cleanse this space,
   No ill may harm, no curse disgrace."

3. Add the Protective Herbs: Add the protective herbs to the bottle, such as rosemary, sage, thyme, and bay leaves. These herbs have long been used in witchcraft to ward off evil and bring protective energy into the home. As you add each herb, focus on its protective properties:

   "By rosemary, sage, and thyme's sweet power,
   I guard my home, by leaf and flower."

4. Add the Black Tourmaline or Obsidian: Place a piece of black tourmaline or obsidian into the bottle for grounding and additional protection. These stones help absorb and neutralize any negative energy. As you add the stone, say:

   "By stone of earth, so dark and strong,
   No ill may stay, no harm belong."

5. Add a Personal Item: Add a small personal item such as a hair strand or nail clipping to connect the bottle directly to you. This will help the bottle protect you specifically, forming a link between your energy and the magic in the bottle.

   "By hair and bone, this spell I weave,
   Protection strong, no harm to grieve."

6. Optional: Add Thorns or Pins: If you want extra strength in your protection, add thorns, pins, or pieces of broken glass to further ward off harmful intentions or spirits.

   "By thorn and shard, by pin and glass,
   I bind all harm, it shall not pass."

Step 3: Sealing the Bottle

1. Seal the Bottle with Wax: Once all the ingredients are inside, close the bottle tightly with its lid. Light a black candle and allow the wax to drip around the edges of the lid, sealing the bottle shut. As you do this, say:

   "By wax and flame, I seal this charm,
   To guard my home from every harm.
   By iron, salt, and stone so pure,
   This magic stands, this spell is sure."

2. Focus on Your Intentions: As the wax seals the bottle, focus on your intention of protection. Visualize the bottle as a powerful shield that absorbs and neutralizes any harmful energy directed at you or your home. See the bottle glowing with protective energy.

Step 4: Hiding the Bottle

1. Bury or Hide the Bottle: To activate the spell, the bottle must be hidden in a discreet place. If you have a yard, bury the bottle near the entrance to your home, or in the four cardinal directions for comprehensive protection. If you don't have outdoor space, you can hide the bottle

in a dark corner of your home, under a threshold, or in a closet. Make sure the bottle remains undisturbed. (If burying, put the bottle in a thick black bag to prevent injury to animals or others.)

2. Reaffirm the Spell: As you place the bottle in its hidden location, say:

"By bottle bound and earth below,
No ill may enter, no harm may flow.
This house is sealed, this charm I cast,
To guard this home, while spell shall last."

Maintaining the Witch's Bottle

The Witch's Bottle is a long-lasting protective charm, but it is good practice to recharge or refresh it periodically. You can do this by sprinkling salt around the area where it's hidden or by performing a cleansing ritual in your home.

The bottle's protective energy will continue to absorb and deflect negativity, keeping your space safe. You can leave it in place for as long as needed, but if the bottle ever breaks or if you feel it has done its job, be sure to dispose of it respectfully – preferably by burying the contents in the earth.

The Witch's Bottle serves as a powerful guardian, protecting you and your home from harm, and creating a barrier of safety against malefic forces

The Bestowal of Spirit

A Ritual to Protect and Consecrate the Witch's Home

In Green Witchcraft, the Bestowal of Spirit is a sacred ritual that transforms your house into more than just a dwelling – it becomes a living entity, a household spirit that protects, empowers, and harmonizes the witch's magic. By naming your home and giving it an identity, you forge a bond with it, ensuring it not only safeguards your physical space but also supports and strengthens your magical workings. This spell involves sweeping the home with the Witch's Broom, placing salt and Full Moon Water in the corners, and positioning four stones charged with Dark Moon Water in the cardinal directions.

This ritual should be cast at least once a month, preferably on the Full Moon or Dark Moon, to maintain the protective and consecrating energy.

You Will Need:

- Your Witch's Broom
- A small bowl of salt (for protection and purification)
- Full Moon Water (for blessing and light)
- Four pieces of Black Tourmaline or Obsidian (for protection, submerged in Dark Moon Water prior to the ritual)
- Optional: White candle (for illumination during the ritual)

Step 1: Naming the House and Bestowing Spirit

1. Stand at the Threshold: Before you begin the ritual, stand at the entrance of your home, either by the front door

or in a central space. Close your eyes and take a few moments to feel the energy of the house. Imagine it as a living entity, waiting for you to recognize it, honor it, and bestow it with a name.

2. Choose a Name: Reflect on the character and spirit of your home. What energy does it carry? What name calls to you as a fitting title for this protective and sacred space? Once the name has revealed itself to you, speak it aloud three times, allowing the energy of the house to respond and acknowledge its new identity.

"By witch's will and spirit's light,
I call your name and give you sight.
By earth, by fire, by water, by air,
[House Name], I call you, live and care."

Step 2: Sweeping the Space with the Witch's Broom

1. Sweep the House: Take your Witch's Broom and, starting at the front door or central space, sweep through the entire home. This act symbolizes clearing out old, stagnant energy and preparing the space for the protective spell. As you sweep, imagine the broom gathering any negative or unwelcome energy and sweeping it out of the house.

"With broom I sweep, with will I clean,
By moon's pure light, I make unseen,
All harm, all ill, all darkness, go,
This house now shines, with sacred glow."

2. Sweep Toward the Exit: Continue sweeping through each room, finishing at a door or window where you can symbolically sweep all negative energy out of the home.

Step 3: Placing Salt and Full Moon Water in the Corners

1. Bless the Corners: In each room of your home, especially at the four cardinal corners of the house, sprinkle a pinch of salt and a few drops of Full Moon Water. These elements represent the earth and water, two foundational elements that purify and protect the space.

"By salt of earth and water bright,
I call protection, pure and light.
No ill shall cross this sacred ground,
My house is safe, my home is bound."

Step 4: Placing the Black Stones in the Cardinal Directions

1. Charge the Stones in Dark Moon Water: Before the ritual, allow the four Black Tourmaline or Obsidian stones to soak in Dark Moon Water. The Dark Moon carries the energy of protection, concealment, and transformation.
2. Place the Stones in the Cardinal Directions: Take each stone and place or bury it at the four cardinal points (North, South, East, and West) around your home. If burying them outside is not possible, position them inside the house as close to the appropriate directions as you can. These stones act as guardians, forming a protective shield around the home. It is essential to keep them unseen and in the dark, ensuring they retain the Dark Moon's magic.

"By stone of night, by moon unseen,
I place you here, to guard between.
In North and South, in East and West,
This house is safe, this home is blessed."

Step 5: Sealing the Ritual of Bestowal of Spirit

1. Seal the Spirit of the House: Stand in the center of your home or at the threshold, holding your Witch's Broom. Visualize the house as a living spirit, connected to you and filled with protective energy. Say the following incantation to seal the Bestowal of Spirit, consecrating the home as a sacred space:

   "By name I call, by spirit true,
   This house now lives, its power new.
   By broom, by salt, by moon's dark light,
   This house protects, by day and night.
   [House Name], rise, your heart now beats,
   Your spirit stands, no ill defeats."

2. Light a White Candle (Optional): If desired, light a white candle to symbolize the illumination of your home's new spirit. Let it burn down safely, as a way to anchor the spirit of the house into the physical space.

Maintaining the Spell: Monthly Recasting

To maintain the protective energy and the Bestowal of Spirit, recast the ritual once a month during either the Full Moon or Dark Moon. Each time, you reaffirm the house's name, sweep the space with your broom, and refresh the salt and moon water in the corners. The stones, kept unseen, continue their work of guarding the boundaries.

Honoring Your Home's Spirit

By naming your home and bestowing upon it an identity, you form a bond between yourself and the space you live in. The house becomes a living entity, a guardian spirit that protects, supports, and empowers your magical workings. Through the Bestowal of Spirit, your home is consecrated, transformed into a temple of magic, where your spells are strengthened, and no ill-intentioned force can enter.

The Power of Names

Imbuing Identity and Purpose in Magical Tools

In the practice of traditional witchcraft, the act of naming carries immense power. It is believed that to give a name is to give identity, to solidify the essence of a person, object, or being. Names, when spoken, hold the ability to shape and direct energy, to focus intent, and to strengthen the connection between the witch and the magical tools they use. This concept applies especially to the witch's personal tools – those sacred items that become extensions of the witch's will.

Why Naming Your Tools Matters

When you name your magical tools, you aren't just assigning them a label – you are invoking their purpose and defining their role in your craft. By naming an athame, broom, cauldron, or any other sacred tool, you call it into its full potential, giving it a unique identity that strengthens its connection to you and your magical practice.

Names carry with them:

- Purpose: When you name a tool, you align it with a specific intention or role. For instance, naming a cauldron could imbue it with the power to hold transformative energy, while naming a broom could deepen its role in protection and cleansing.
- Identity: Just as a name gives identity to people, it gives identity to objects. A named tool becomes a living part of your magical world, distinct and powerful.
- Connection: By naming a tool, you forge a personal bond with it. This bond makes your interactions with the tool more meaningful and strengthens the tool's effectiveness in your spells and rituals.

- Empowerment: The act of naming is an act of empowerment. It activates the latent energy in the tool and calls it to serve with focus and intention. A named tool becomes more than just a material object – it becomes a partner in your magic.

How to Name Your Tools

Naming a tool should be a sacred act, done with care and intention. The process can be simple or elaborate, depending on your personal preference, but the key is to focus on the energy and purpose of the tool when you choose its name.

1. Connect with the Tool: Spend time with the tool before naming it. Hold it in your hands, focus on its shape and weight, and consider how you plan to use it. Meditate on its energy and allow its purpose to become clear.
2. Choose a Meaningful Name: The name you choose should reflect the essence of the tool. You can draw from nature, mythology, or personal experiences. The name could be a word that represents the tool's power (like "Blade of Shadows" for an athame) or something symbolic of its role in your magic (like "Windward" for a broom used in wind or air spells).
3. Speak the Name: Once you've chosen a name, speak it aloud to the tool, breathing life into its identity. As you say the name, visualize the tool glowing with energy, now fully imbued with its purpose.
4. Seal the Name in Ritual: After naming the tool, perform a small ritual to seal the name. You can anoint the tool with Full Moon Water or Dark Moon Water, surround it with herbs, or place it on your altar while reciting

an incantation. This ritual solidifies the connection between you and the tool, ensuring that the name carries power.

Example Ritual for Naming a Tool

1. Prepare the Space: Light a candle (white for general magic, black for protection, or a color that corresponds to the tool's purpose). Place the tool on your altar, along with herbs, crystals, or moon water to amplify its energy.
2. Hold the Tool: Pick up the tool and focus on its energy. Meditate on the purpose of the tool and the role it will play in your magic.
3. Speak the Name: Once you feel connected to the tool, say its chosen name three times. As you speak, visualize the tool glowing with energy. Feel the bond forming between you and the tool.

"By this name, I call you forth,
Your purpose clear, your power true.
With this name, I bind our bond,
In moonlight's glow, in shadow's hue."

4. Seal the Name: Sprinkle the tool with Full Moon Water or anoint it with oil as you recite an incantation to seal the name:

"By water clear and flame alight,
I seal this name, with power bright.
In magic's realm, this tool shall stand,
Its name known true, by witch's hand."

5. Close the Ritual: Allow the tool to rest on your altar until the candle burns out, solidifying the energy of its new name.

The Power of Names in Spellcraft

Names are not only important for tools but also for the spells and rituals you perform. By naming a spell, you give it a distinct identity and purpose, helping to focus your energy and intention. The name of a spell acts as a key, unlocking its power each time you invoke it.

For example, naming a spell "The Bound Winds" immediately gives it form and clarity, allowing the magic to align with the will of the witch. When you create spells or charms, take the time to name them thoughtfully, as it will help to empower the magic and give the spell a distinct presence in your practice.

The Sacred Act of Naming

In magic, naming is an act of creation. By giving a name, you breathe life into an object, spell, or tool, imbuing it with identity and purpose. This is why naming your magical tools is so important – it transforms them from simple objects into partners in your craft, each carrying a unique energy that enhances your spells and rituals. A tool with a name is a tool with power, and by invoking that name, you activate the tool's full potential, aligning it with your will and the magic you create.

Deep Magic Consecration: A Theory of Magic

The secret of both Deep and High Magic is the clarity and strength of will of the witch. The ingredients, the incantations, the carefully chosen correspondences, and the elaborate rituals are all tools that serve to empower the one essential element: the intention and engagement of the invoking witch. Without this singular focus, these external elements are mere symbols, inert and hollow. The true power lies in the will – the concentrated force that moves the energies of the universe.

In ancient times, rituals demanded an intensity of passion and a full immersion of the self. The witch entered states of heightened emotional and spiritual ecstasy, transcending the ordinary and channeling their desires into the fabric of reality. It was through this fervor that magic became real, that the unseen forces answered the call of human will. Our modern minds, however, struggle to reach that passionate intensity. We are surrounded by distractions, noise, and skepticism. For us, the use of incantations and rituals serves to guide our mind into a state of focus, a state where belief outweighs doubt.

Magic is most powerful when you are in an emotionally heightened state, when your doubts are silenced, and your intention is clear. In those moments – whether in the dark wood or under the shadow of the moon – you trust your feet to step across the root-laden floor, moving instinctively in rhythm with your purpose. You are no longer just performing a spell; you become the spell. The deeper the emotional engagement, the stronger the magic, as the witch's will aligns completely with the forces they seek to invoke. This is where true magic thrives.

The Power of Intention

At the core of all magic is intention – focused, unwavering, and clear. Intention drives every aspect of the spell, shaping energy into action. When the witch's will is sharp and undistracted, magic flows naturally, aligning with the desired outcome. In moments where doubt has no place, the witch becomes one with their purpose, and the forces of magic answer with precision.

Imagine standing in the forest under the moon, where the veil between the worlds feels thin. The air is thick with mystery, and the ground beneath you hums with ancient life. In this space, there is no room for hesitation. Your will must move like an arrow, direct and purposeful. Your entire being becomes a channel for the energy you summon. The heightened state of emotion and full trust in your path combine to create the spark of magic, a force that can reshape reality.

Rituals as Psychological Keys

For the modern witch, conditioned by logic and reason, it can be difficult to reach the intense emotional states that once fueled ancient rites. This is why rituals, incantations, and correspondences remain vital. They serve as psychological keys, guiding us into a state of focus where the mind aligns with intention. Each word, each gesture, and each ingredient is chosen not for its own power, but because it helps focus the mind and spirit on the work at hand.

A rose may symbolize love, but its real power lies in the emotional resonance it holds within the witch. The symbols, herbs, and incantations we use are deeply personal and act as bridges between our conscious and subconscious minds, between the physical and the spiritual. The more we believe in these symbols, the more effectively they serve as conduits for our will. Ritual, then, becomes not just a set of actions but a way to immerse ourselves fully in the magical process, amplifying our will through layers of meaning and emotional connection.

Emotion as a Catalyst

The emotional state of the witch is crucial to the success of any spell. Magic thrives in states of emotional intensity – whether born from passion, grief, love, or even rage. The deeper the emotional investment, the more energy is aligned with the spell's intention. When emotion and will flow together, the barriers of doubt dissolve, and the magic becomes a living force.

This is why magic is most potent in moments of emotional height, when the witch feels alive and connected to the deepest parts of their being. In these moments, the witch becomes the embodiment of their desire. The emotional energy acts as a catalyst, fueling the spell and drawing in the forces needed for its manifestation. When the heart and mind are fully engaged, magic flows naturally, aligning the inner will with the outer world.

The Green Witch and the Power of Nature

For the Green Witch, strengthening will and intention goes beyond ritual – it is nurtured through deep communion with the natural world. The Green Witch finds their power in the wild places, in the silence of woodland groves, and the quiet expanses of meadows. By exploring nature, by sitting in the stillness of the trees or the song of the wind, the Green Witch attunes themselves to the cycles of the earth. The deep magic of nature speaks in the rustling leaves, the flowing water, and the rise and fall of the sun. Here, the Green Witch learns the rhythms that guide all life, and in that understanding, strengthens their own will.

Gardening and tending plants is also a spiritual practice for the Green Witch. In the simple act of planting seeds and nurturing their growth, the witch experiences the miracle of the soil and the seed, the unfolding mystery of life itself. They learn patience, trust, and the power of the cycle. The rose that sleeps beneath the snow and resurrects in the spring teaches the witch that magic, like nature, follows a sacred rhythm of death and rebirth. Each flower that blooms, each herb that thrives under their care, is a reflection of the witch's will made manifest in the world.

Tending the earth strengthens the Green Witch's connection to the forces they invoke. The act of gardening, of caring for plants and watching them grow, teaches the witch about the slow and sacred process of creation. Just as the climbing rose finds its way upward, seeking the light, the Green Witch cultivates their will – steady, strong, and reaching. The cycles of nature become the framework for the witch's own power, for magic is not separate from the world, but woven into its very fabric. In nature's patterns, the witch sees their own, knowing that their will, like the seed, will bloom in its time.

The Shadow of the Moon

There is a reason witches have long been associated with the moon and the night. The deep, the unknown, and the wild places call to the instinctual parts of us that understand magic without needing to rationalize it. In the shadow of the moon, where the boundaries between the seen and unseen blur, magic thrives. In these moments, the witch becomes attuned to the rhythm of the world, stepping into a liminal space where their will can shape reality.

In the deep woods or beneath the stars, when the witch moves instinctively, trusting their feet to step across the forest floor, they are in communion with the unseen. In this state, magic is not something they do – it is something they are. The witch becomes a living embodiment of their will, channeling the forces of the earth and sky to manifest their desire.

Conclusion: The Witch as the Source of Power

Magic, in its essence, is the art of focusing and directing energy through the power of will. The deeper the engagement of the witch, the stronger the magic. It is the clarity of intention and the ability to enter an emotionally heightened state that defines successful spellwork. The tools, symbols, and rituals are powerful because they help the witch reach the place of pure intention and emotional connection. But it is the witch's own will, undiluted and unwavering, that is the true source of magic's power.

For the Green Witch, this power is intimately tied to their connection with nature. Through tending plants, walking in wild places, and observing the cycles of life, the Green Witch learns to cultivate their will as they cultivate the earth. Just as a climbing rose seeks the light, so too does the witches will grow, strong and steady, guided by the rhythms of nature. It is in this union between the witch and the wild that true magic is born.

In the end, Deep and High Magic are not defined by the complexity of rituals or the rarity of ingredients, but by the simplicity of focused intention. The witch is the center of this power, standing at the nexus of the physical and spiritual, drawing forth from the depths of their own will to create change in the world. And it is in those moments of heightened clarity, when doubt fades and the soul aligns with purpose, that true magic is born.

General Tips for Adapting Spells

1. Change Herbs Based on Intent: Each herb carries its own unique magical properties. If you're seeking a different outcome, choose herbs that correspond with your new purpose. For example, basil for prosperity, lavender for calm, rose for love, and rosemary for protection.
2. Alter Incantations: Words have power, so rework your incantation to reflect the new intention. Be clear and specific about what you're asking for.
3. Use Different Tools: Swap out materials that correspond with different elements or energies. For example, use crystals like rose quartz for love, citrine for abundance, or obsidian for protection.
4. Focus on the Moon Phases: Adapt your timing to the moon's phases. For example:

- Dark Moon concealment and shadow work.
- New Moon for new beginnings and growth.
- Waxing Moon for manifesting and bringing things into your life.
- Full Moon for power and completion.
- Waning Moon for releasing or banishing.

By making these adjustments, you can tailor the spells in your spellbook to align with your specific goals, needs, and the type of energy you want to harness. Keep experimenting and trust your intuition as you create a practice that feels personal and powerful to you.

Restorative Tea of the Grove

Adaptation: From Balance to Motivation and Energy

You can easily adapt this tea for increasing energy, focus, or motivation.

Herb Substitutions:

- Replace **lemon balm** with **peppermint** or **green tea** for an energizing boost.
- Add **ginger** and **cinnamon** for warmth and extra vitality.

New Incantation:

"By fire and root, by leaf and light,
Grant me energy, sharp and bright.
With every sip, strength is mine,
Focus clear and spirit aligned."

Green Witch's Hair Gloss

Adaptation: From Hair Care to Spiritual Cleansing

This gloss can be adapted into a ritual for cleansing and refreshing your spiritual energy or aura.

Materials Adaptation:

- Swap the rosemary with sage or lavender for spiritual cleansing.
- Infuse the oil with frankincense essential oil to promote spiritual protection and purification.

New Incantation:

"By herb and oil, I now remove,
All energy that does not improve.

With cleansing force, I clear my way,
Spirits high, as bright as day."

Wildflower Dream Pillow

Adaptation: From Dream Enhancement to Protection During Sleep

Instead of focusing on enhancing dreams, you can adapt this pillow for protection during sleep or to ward off nightmares.

Herb Substitutions:

- Add mugwort (for protection during sleep) and bay leaves (for banishing nightmares).
- Replace the amethyst with black tourmaline or obsidian for additional protection.

New Incantation:

"By herb and stone, I banish fear,
No harm or dread shall enter here.
As I sleep, I rest with ease,
Safe and sound, protected by these."

Talisman of the Stag

Adaptation: From Strength to Fertility or Growth

You can adapt the talisman's purpose from strength and protection to fertility, growth (personal, spiritual, or physical), or even creativity.

Materials Adaptation:

- Include a small **acorn** (symbolizing new beginnings and growth) or **apple seeds** (representing fertility).

- Infuse it with herbs like **basil** (for fertility) or **sunflower seeds** (for personal growth).

New Incantation:

"By seed and wood, by fertile ground,
I call forth growth, pure and sound.
Through nature's grace, new life shall spring,
Blessed by the wild, I now bring."

Traditional Herbs in Green Witchcraft

Rosemary

- Magical Properties: Protection, cleansing, clarity, memory
- Uses: Rosemary is one of the most versatile herbs in Green Witchcraft. It is often burned to cleanse spaces, used in protection spells, and incorporated into rituals to enhance memory and mental clarity. Witches also use it in bath rituals for purification.

Lavender

- Magical Properties: Peace, calm, love, healing
- Uses: Lavender is used in spells to promote peace and relaxation, and to bring calm into a space or a person's energy. It's also common in love spells and healing rituals. The soothing scent can be used to help with sleep or to create a sense of calm in stressful environments.

Sage

- Magical Properties: Cleansing, wisdom, protection
- Uses: Sage is a traditional herb used for cleansing and purifying spaces, objects, and people. In Green Witchcraft, sage is often burned (smudged) to banish negative energies, to protect from harm, or to promote wisdom and clarity in decision-making.

Thyme

- Magical Properties: Courage, healing, protection

- Uses: Thyme is a powerful herb used for courage and strength. It's often included in healing rituals and spells designed to protect and fortify both the body and spirit. Thyme can also be used in bath magic for invigoration and health.

Mugwort

- Magical Properties: Psychic abilities, dreamwork, protection
- Uses: Mugwort is deeply connected to psychic abilities and is often used in spells and rituals to enhance intuition, prophetic dreams, and divination. It is also burned or carried to protect from harmful spirits and energies.

Dandelion

- Magical Properties: Wishes, divination, spirit communication
- Uses: The dandelion is often used in spells for wish-making and manifestation. Its seeds, when blown into the wind, carry wishes. Dandelion roots can be used in teas or carried as a charm for divination and connecting with the spirit world.

Chamomile

- Magical Properties: Calm, peace, sleep, love
- Uses: Chamomile is a gentle yet powerful herb in Green Witchcraft, used to bring peace, calm, and emotional healing. It's often used in sleep spells, dream pillows, and soothing teas. Chamomile is also used in spells to attract love and friendship.

Nettle

- Magical Properties: Protection, healing, strength
- Uses: Nettle is often used in protection spells and to ward off negativity. Its powerful energy also supports healing and strengthening spells. In Green Witchcraft, nettle is associated with building personal resilience and power.

Yarrow

- Magical Properties: Courage, protection, love
- Uses: Yarrow is a traditional herb for courage, particularly when facing personal challenges. It's used in spells for protection, especially in guarding the heart. It's also associated with love and is often used in love spells and charm bags.

Basil

- Magical Properties: Prosperity, protection, love
- Uses: Basil is often used in Green Witchcraft to bring prosperity and abundance, both material and spiritual. It's a protective herb that can guard against negative energy, and it's frequently included in love spells to foster harmony and fidelity.

Mint

- Magical Properties: Healing, prosperity, purification
- Uses: Mint is used to refresh and invigorate energy, often in healing and prosperity spells. It's also used to purify spaces and clear away stagnant energy. Mint leaves are often carried in charm bags for good luck and abundance.

Elder (Elderberry or Elderflower)

- Magical Properties: Protection, healing, warding off spirits
- Uses: Elder is one of the most sacred trees in Green Witchcraft. Its berries and flowers are used in protection spells and to guard against malevolent spirits. It's also used in healing rituals and to promote health and well-being.

Hawthorn

- Magical Properties: Protection, love, fertility
- Uses: Hawthorn is a protective and sacred herb that's often associated with the fae and the Otherworld. It's used in protection spells, fertility rites, and to promote love and harmony in relationships. It is also often planted around homes as a protective boundary.

Vervain

- Magical Properties: Purification, protection, love
- Uses: Vervain is a highly magical herb traditionally used in rituals for purification and protection. It's believed to be especially effective against harmful spirits. Vervain is also used in love spells and rituals to attract romance and passion.

Rue

- Magical Properties: Protection, banishing, healing
- Uses: Rue is often used for its strong protective and cleansing properties. It's used to banish negative energies, break curses, and protect the witch from harm. Rue can also be included in healing spells for physical and emotional ailments.

Table of Correspondences

Herbs

Herb	Correspondence	Use For
Basil	Prosperity, protection, love	Wealth, attracting abundance
Lavender	Calm, healing, love	Stress relief, love, peace
Rosemary	Protection, cleansing, memory	Protection spells, mental clarity
Peppermint	Energy, clarity, purification	Energizing, clarity of mind
Chamomile	Relaxation, peace, healing	Calming anxiety, emotional healing
Sage	Purification, wisdom, protection	Cleansing spaces, banishing negativity
Cinnamon	Success, passion, speed	Success spells, quick manifestation
Mugwort	Psychic awareness, protection	Dreamwork, divination, protection
Nettle	Strength, healing, courage	Personal strength, protection spells
Elderflower	Beauty, protection, healing	Skin care, personal beauty rituals
Bay Leaf	Manifestation, protection, psychic ability	Wishing spells, warding off nightmares
Thyme	Courage, healing, purification	Health spells, boosting courage
Calendula	Healing, protection, legal matters	Physical healing, emotional protection
Rose Petals	Love, attraction, harmony	Self-love, romantic intentions
Ginger	Power, love, vitality	Increasing energy, motivation, passion

Crystals

Crystal	Correspondence	Use For
Clear Quartz	Amplification, clarity, energy	Enhancing spell energy, clarity of intent
Amethyst	Spirituality, protection, intuition	Meditation, psychic abilities, dreams
Rose Quartz	Love, compassion, emotional healing	Self-love, relationships, healing hearts
Citrine	Abundance, creativity, success	Prosperity, success, manifesting goals
Black Tourmaline	Protection, grounding, warding off negativity	Personal protection, shielding spells
Obsidian	Protection, grounding, removing negativity	Banishing, clearing negative energy
Moonstone	Intuition, emotional balance, new beginnings	Dreamwork, cycles of change, fertility
Carnelian	Courage, energy, creativity	Increasing motivation, personal power
Tiger's Eye	Courage, protection, willpower	Boosting confidence, grounding energy
Selenite	Cleansing, protection, spiritual work	Cleansing rituals, psychic protection
Labradorite	Transformation, protection, psychic powers	Heightening intuition, spiritual protection
Jade	Luck, health, prosperity	Attracting wealth, improving health

Colors

Color	Correspondence	Use For
White	Purity, protection, cleansing	General protection, purification, clarity
Black	Banishing, protection, grounding	Removing negativity, protection rituals
Green	Growth, abundance, healing	Health, prosperity, fertility
Red	Passion, vitality, strength	Love spells, courage, motivation
Blue	Peace, communication, healing	Calm, emotional healing, truth-speaking
Yellow	Creativity, confidence, mental clarity	Success, joy, stimulating creativity
Purple	Psychic ability, wisdom, spirituality	Spiritual work, dream magic, intuition
Gold	Success, wealth, power	Attracting abundance, victory spells
Silver	Intuition, moon magic, feminine energy	Psychic work, cycles, lunar spells

Elements

Element	Correspondence	Use For
Air	Communication, intellect, clarity	Mental clarity, communication spells
Fire	Transformation, passion, energy	Courage, motivation, swift action
Water	Emotions, intuition, healing	Emotional healing, dreams, psychic work
Earth	Grounding, stability, fertility	Prosperity, protection, health, growth
Spirit	Connection to the divine, the unknown	Spiritual growth, divine guidance

Moon Phases

Moon Phase	Correspondence	Use For
New Moon	New beginnings, planting seeds	Initiating new projects, setting intentions
Waxing Moon	Growth, expansion, attraction	Manifesting desires, increasing prosperity
Full Moon	Power, completion, heightened energy	Powerful spellwork, fulfillment of goals
Waning Moon	Release, banishment, letting go	Clearing away negativity, ending bad habits
Dark Moon	Rest, reflection, mystery	Deep introspection, banishing, transformation

Planets

Planet	Correspondence	Use For
Sun	Vitality, success, leadership	Success, energy, confidence
Moon	Emotions, intuition, cycles	Dream magic, emotional healing, change
Mercury	Communication, intellect, travel	Mental clarity, business, travel spells
Venus	Love, beauty, relationships	Love spells, beauty, attraction
Mars	Strength, passion, conflict resolution	Courage, action, breaking barriers
Jupiter	Abundance, expansion, wisdom	Prosperity, success, knowledge
Saturn	Discipline, protection, structure	Long-term goals, protection, boundaries
Uranus	Change, innovation, freedom	Breakthroughs, unexpected changes
Neptune	Dreams, spirituality, intuition	Dream work, psychic abilities, creativity
Pluto	Transformation, death, rebirth	Deep transformation, shadow work

Using the Correspondences

To adapt a spell, choose elements from the table that match your specific intention. For example, if you're adapting a beauty spell to focus on attracting love:

- Herbs: Swap rosemary (protection) with rose petals (love) or lavender (peace and love).
- Crystals: Replace clear quartz (general amplification) with rose quartz for self-love or romantic attraction.
- Colors: Use pink or red candles or ribbons to symbolize love and passion.
- Moon Phase: Perform the spell during the Waxing Moon to increase the love or attraction you seek.

If you want to adapt a protection spell to focus on prosperity:

- Herbs: Use basil or cinnamon to draw wealth and abundance.
- Crystals: Incorporate citrine or green aventurine for prosperity and success.
- Colors: Choose green or gold candles to represent wealth and financial growth.
- Element: Focus on Earth to ground and stabilize the wealth you're attracting.

Step-by-Step Adaptation: Protection to Love Spell

1. **Adjust the Intention**

In a protection spell, the focus is on shielding yourself from harm or negativity. To shift this toward love, your intention should focus on attracting love, self-love, or fostering a harmonious relationship. Think about the type of love you want to attract (self-love, romantic love, or friendship), and set a clear intention.

Example of Adapted Intention:
Instead of, "I protect myself from harm," focus on something like:

> *"I invite love into my life, filled with harmony, passion, and joy."*

2. Swap Out Protective Herbs for Love Herbs

Protection spells often use herbs like rosemary, sage, or juniper for their protective qualities. To focus on love, switch these to herbs traditionally associated with attraction, harmony, or romance.

Herbs for Love:

- Rose petals (for love and romance)
- Lavender (for peace and love)
- Basil (for harmony and fidelity in relationships)
- Cinnamon (for passion and attraction)
- Jasmine (for sensuality and romantic love)
- Catnip (to attract a lover or enhance flirtation)
- Damiana (for passion and intimacy)

3. Change Crystals

Protection spells often use stones like black tourmaline or obsidian for their shielding properties. For a love-focused spell, switch to crystals that attract love and foster emotional connection.

Crystals for Love:

- Rose Quartz (for self-love and attracting love)
- Garnet (for passion and commitment)
- Rhodonite (for emotional healing and love)
- Moonstone (for romance and emotional balance)
- Pink Tourmaline (for emotional healing and love)

4. Adapt the Incantation

The incantation of a protection spell is typically about banishing harm or creating a protective barrier. For love, your incantation should call in loving energies, emotional connection, or self-love.

Example of Adapted Incantation:

Instead of saying, "No harm shall come near me," shift it to something like:

> *"By rose and light, love I call near,*
> *With passion and joy, I hold it dear.*
> *By nature's grace and moon's soft glow,*
> *Love blooms within, and out it grows."*

5. Use Corresponding Colors

Protection spells often use colors like black or white for warding off negativity. For love, use colors that align with romance and attraction.

Colors for Love:

- Pink (for love, compassion, and harmony)
- Red (for passion, desire, and physical attraction)

- Green (for growth and emotional connection)
- White (for purity and peace in relationships)

6. Add Symbolic Elements

Consider adding symbols of love, such as:

- Candles: Use pink or red candles to represent love and attraction.
- Flowers: Place roses or fresh flowers around your space to invite in loving energy.
- Charm or Talisman: Add a charm like a heart-shaped pendant or something personal to you that represents love.

Example of an Adapted Spell: Attracting Love

You Will Need:

- Rose petals or lavender (for love and peace)
- Cinnamon (for passion and attraction)
- Rose quartz crystal (for self-love and attracting love)
- A pink or red candle
- A small piece of paper and pen
- A few drops of rose oil (optional)

Instructions:

1. Set Your Intention: Begin by taking a few moments to ground yourself. Visualize the type of love you want to attract – be it romantic, self-love, or a deeper connection with others. Keep your mind focused on this intention throughout the ritual.

2. Prepare Your Space: Light the pink or red candle. Place the rose petals (or lavender) and cinnamon in a small dish, and hold the rose quartz crystal in your hand. As you arrange your space, invite loving, peaceful energy to flow into the circle.
3. Write Your Intention: On the small piece of paper, write down your intention. For example:

"I attract love into my life, filling my heart with joy, compassion, and passion."

4. Infuse Your Ingredients with Energy: As you sprinkle the rose petals and cinnamon around the candle, say:

"By rose and spice, I call to me,
Love that flows like the endless sea."
Hold the rose quartz and continue:
"With crystal clear, love now grows,
In this heart, pure love shall flow."

5. Burn the Intention: Take your piece of paper and hold it over the candle flame (safely). As it burns, visualize your desire for love manifesting in your life. See yourself surrounded by loving energy and happiness.
6. Close the Spell: Once the paper has burned, take a moment to feel gratitude for the love that is coming into your life. Snuff out the candle and keep the rose quartz on your altar or near your bed as a reminder of the spell's energy.

New Incantation:

"By rose and light, love I call near,
With passion and joy, I hold it dear.

By nature's grace and moon's soft glow,
Love blooms within, and out it grows."

Other Tips for Adapting Protection to Love:

- Change the Focus of Your Visualization: Instead of visualizing a protective barrier around yourself, picture yourself radiating love and warmth, attracting positive relationships or romantic connections.
- Shift the Energy of the Ritual Space: Instead of cleansing the space with sage or rosemary for protection, try using rosewater or lavender oil to create a loving, peaceful atmosphere.
- Moon Phase: Perform the spell during the Waxing Moon to draw love toward you, or on the Full Moon to amplify the spell's energy.

Acknowledgments

The spells, rituals, and incantations in this collection are rooted in the rich history of Traditional Witchcraft and draw on diverse traditions that honor the natural world, the elements, and the spirits. Influenced by folk magic, Hedge Witchcraft, and Green Witchcraft, these original spells are infused with a deep respect for the practices of witches who worked closely with the cycles of nature and the rhythms of the earth.

In particular, I honor the following traditions and sources that have contributed to the creation of this grimoire:

Traditional Witchcraft: This collection's foundational practices of old-world magic are woven throughout this collection. Traditional Witchcraft's focus on sympathetic magic, the power of the moon, and the use of the elements to manifest intentions form the core of many spells within this grimoire.

Hedge Witchcraft: The concept of crossing the hedge – the boundary between the physical and spiritual worlds – is central to many of the spells here, particularly those that involve spirit communication, such as the Feast of the Spirits. Hedge Witchcraft's emphasis on walking between worlds mirrors the deep connection between the witch and the unseen realms.

Green Witchcraft: Green Witchcraft's focus on working in harmony with nature, foraging for natural materials, and connecting deeply with the elements is reflected in many of the spells. Herb magic, elemental spells, and the reverence for the land and its cycles are integral parts of this magical system.

Cornish Witchcraft: The influence of Cornish magic can be seen in the use of storm summoning, knot magic, and the intimate relationship with the forces of land and sea. Cornish witches were known for their ability to work with the elements and the natural world to bring about change, a practice that is honored in this grimoire.

Hecate and the Goddess Traditions: The invocation of Hecate, the Goddess of Witches, speaks to her timeless role in Witchcraft as the guide of souls, the keeper of crossroads, and the protector of witches. Spells like the Feast of the Spirits draw on her ancient power as the Guardian of the Dead and the Mistress of Mysteries.

Folk Magic: The simplicity and practicality of folk magic are present throughout this collection, particularly in the use of herbs, charms, and knot spells. Folk magic has always been about using what is at hand, finding the magic in the everyday, and that spirit continues in the spells presented here.

The Lattice of the Twin Moons

The Twin Moons system, or The Lattice of The Twin Moons, as presented in this grimoire, is a wholly original creation and comes from the personal practice of the grimoire's author. It is based on the dual nature of the moon – the Full Moon as a source of radiant power and protection and the Dark Moon as a veil of shadow and concealment. This system reflects the belief that light and darkness are essential forces in the natural world, and by invoking both aspects of the Twin Moons, the witch can balance these energies and harness their power for a wide variety of spells.

MOON BOOKS

PAGANISM & SHAMANISM

What is Paganism? A religion, a spirituality, an alternative belief system, nature worship? You can find support for all these definitions (and many more) in dictionaries, encyclopaedias, and text books of religion, but subscribe to any one and the truth will evade you. Above all Paganism is a creative pursuit, an encounter with reality, an exploration of meaning and an expression of the soul. Druids, Heathens, Wiccans and others, all contribute their insights and literary riches to the Pagan tradition. Moon Books invites you to begin or to deepen your own encounter, right here, right now.

If you have enjoyed this book, why not tell other readers by posting a review on your preferred book site.

Bestsellers from Moon Books

Keeping Her Keys
An Introduction to Hekate's Modern Witchcraft
Cyndi Brannen
Blending Hekate, witchcraft and personal development together to create
a powerful new magickal perspective.
Paperback: 978-1-78904-075-3 ebook 978-1-78904-076-0

Journey to the Dark Goddess
How to Return to Your Soul
Jane Meredith
Discover the powerful secrets of the Dark Goddess and transform your depression, grief and pain into healing and integration.
Paperback: 978-1-84694-677-6 ebook: 978-1-78099-223-5

Shamanic Reiki
Expanded Ways of Working with Universal Life Force Energy
Llyn Roberts, Robert Levy
Shamanism and Reiki are each powerful ways of healing; together, their power multiplies. Shamanic Reiki introduces techniques to help healers and Reiki practitioners tap ancient healing wisdom.
Paperback: 978-1-84694-037-8 ebook: 978-1-84694-650-9

Southern Cunning
Folkloric Witchcraft in the American South
Aaron Oberon
Modern witchcraft with a Southern flair, this book is a journey through the folklore of the American South and a look at the power these stories hold for modern witches.
Paperback: 978-1-78904-196-5 ebook: 978-1-78904-197-2

Bestsellers from Moon Books
Pagan Portals Series

The Morrigan

Meeting the Great Queens

Morgan Daimler

Ancient and enigmatic, the Morrigan reaches out to us. On shadowed wings and in raven's call, meet the ancient Irish goddess of war, battle, prophecy, death, sovereignty, and magic.

Paperback: 978-1-78279-833-0 ebook: 978-1-78279-834-7

The Awen Alone

Walking the Path of the Solitary Druid

Joanna van der Hoeven

An introductory guide for the solitary Druid, The Awen Alone will accompany you as you explore, and seek out your own place within the natural world.

Paperback: 978-1-78279-547-6 ebook: 978-1-78279-546-9

Moon Magic

Rachel Patterson

An introduction to working with the phases of the Moon, what they are and how to live in harmony with the lunar year and to utilise all the magical powers it provides.

Paperback: 978-1-78279-281-9 ebook: 978-1-78279-282-6

Hekate

A Devotional

Vivienne Moss

Hekate, Queen of Witches and the Shadow-Lands, haunts the pages of this devotional bringing magic and enchantment into your lives

Paperback: 978-1-78535-161-7 ebook: 978-1-78535-162-4

Readers of ebooks can buy or view any of these bestsellers by clicking on the live link in the title. Most titles are published in paperback and as an ebook. Paperbacks are available in traditional bookshops. Both print and ebook formats are available online.

Find more titles and sign up to our readers' newsletter
www.collectiveinkbooks.com/paganism

For video content, author interviews and more, please subscribe to our YouTube channel.

MoonBooksPublishing

Follow us on social media for book news, promotions and more:

Facebook: Moon Books

Instagram: @MoonBooksCI

X: @MoonBooksCI

TikTok: @MoonBooksCI